THE NATURALIST IN MAJORCA

In the same series

THE NATURALIST IN WALES
by R. M. Lockley

THE NATURALIST IN DEVON
AND CORNWALL
by Roger Burrows

THE NATURALIST IN THE ISLE OF MAN
by Larch S. Garrad

THE NATURALIST IN
CENTRAL SOUTHERN ENGLAND
by Derrick Knowlton

THE NATURALIST IN
Majorca

JAMES D. PARRACK

DAVID & CHARLES : NEWTON ABBOT

0 7153 5948 7

Set in 12 on 13pt Bembo
and printed in Great Britain
by Latimer Trend & Company Ltd Plymouth
for David & Charles (Holdings) Limited
South Devon House Newton Abbot Devon

To my wife Anne, who, by reason of a honeymoon or some-thing, was in part responsible for first introducing me to the Balearics. She is one of the original druids, but nobly sacrificed many hours of sun-worship in the cause of chasing across impossible terrain after some elusive insect, or driving the little Seat 600 along even more impossible roads whilst being continually exhorted to stop! go faster! follow that bird! and various other even less practicable and often unprintable alternatives. Add to this her highly competent specialist treatment of numerous attacks of 'predator-watcher's neck', and what more could any man ask?

Contents

List of Illustrations

Plates

Preface

ON MANY OCCASIONS in recent years, I have received requests for information on the ornithology and other aspects of the natural history of Majorca, and these requests have almost invariably been accompanied by comments on the scarcity of available information. There are, it is true, a number of fairly comprehensive specialist contributions in various continental languages, but the material generally at the disposal of the casual British visitor is scant. Apart from the few well-illustrated but not very comprehensive Mediterranean and European floras, and the invaluable Collins' (and other) Field Guides, there is little of real use at an acceptable price.

In view of the steadily increasing number of naturalists of all persuasions now holidaying in Majorca, it soon became evident that there was a real demand for a semi-technical work that would be of use to the collector, student and casual holiday-maker alike. As it had been my original intention to concentrate on an ornithological checklist only, I approached the project of a more comprehensive volume with no little trepidation, as I venture to think would anyone faced with such a task single-handed. In some fields (notably when dealing with some of the more difficult orders of insects containing many rare, endemic species) I had to rely heavily in the initial stages on the work of Colom, whose excellent book copiously illustrated with beautifully accurate line drawings (albeit written in Spanish) is readily available in Palma. This book deserves to be more widely known, and is really a 'must' for all serious naturalists visiting the island, entomologists in particular.

Once the project got under way, however, it was amazing

how information began to roll in. The sources are too numerous to mention, but I must single out the assistance given by friends and acquaintances working with the BBC Natural History Unit at Bristol, who provided many out-of-the-way ornithological and other records, all of which proved invaluable in helping to complete the picture. Inevitably there will be gaps and (though I hope not many) inaccuracies: some work has had to be based on the notes of collectors of bygone years, and though they no doubt did a thorough job, evolution is a continuous process, and can be seen to work particularly rapidly in areas where man can be accused of too active interference with the environment. Conditions change, and the science of ecology—relating living things to their environment—though pioneered by Aristotle some 2,500 years ago in the days of Ancient Greece, has been slow to develop.

Indeed it was a combination of the need to collate what is known, together with a desire to draw attention to the shortcomings in our knowledge that need to be filled before adequate conservation measures can be introduced, that eventually decided me to embark on what has proved to be a most fascinating and rewarding study—the compilation of this book. I can only hope that the reader finds equal pleasure in absorbing it, and makes it his companion in exploring the many still delightfully unspoilt areas of this lovely holiday island.

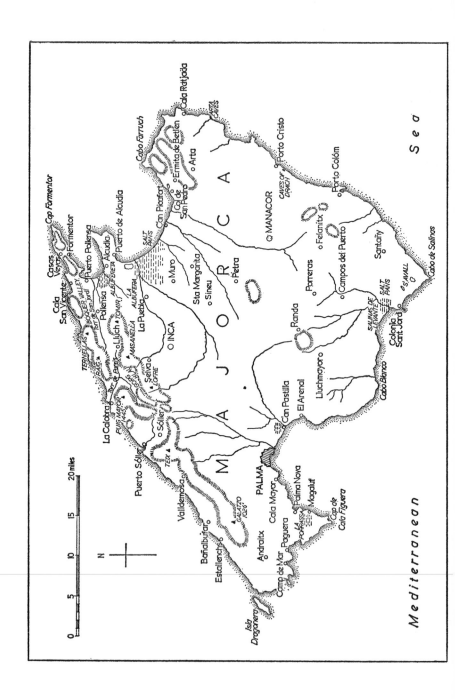

CHAPTER ONE

Majorca – its scenery, character and people

MAJORCA IS THE largest of the islands of the Balearic group, having an area of some 1,405sq miles (3,650sq km). It possesses the most magnificent scenery, and supports the greatest variety of plant and animal life of all the islands, besides being the best known as a holiday resort and consequently the most accessible. The other members of the group in order of decreasing size are Minorca, Ibiza, Formentera and Cabrera, whilst in addition there are numerous offshore islets, many of which (due to long isolation from their neighbours) have developed very interesting indigenous fauna and flora, so that despite their small size they are by no means negligible from the point of view of the naturalist.

Partly due to its greater size, but also as a result of various geological and structural factors to be discussed later, Majorca offers a greater variety of habitat than do the other islands. Moreover, these different habitats or biotopes have succeeded in retaining their individuality to a remarkable degree, with in many cases quite clearly defined boundaries. As a result the amateur ecologist has ample facilities for the study of individual communities and their development relatively unhindered by intrusive elements from neighbouring communities.

Another notable feature of the natural history of Majorca is that many of these biological associations occur within easy reach of each other, the whole island measuring only some 56 by 40 miles (90km by 65km). The tremendous scope the island offers can be seen from the fact that a naturalist based at Pto de

Pollensa has within easy reach the coastal dunes of the littoral belt, the mixed salt- and fresh-water marshes of the Albufera of Alcudia (with its salt-pans) and the Albufereta of Pollensa, garigue vegetation of three distinct types, lowland pinewoods, coastal cliffs of over 1,300ft (400m) altitude, orchards and olive-groves, mountain woodlands of pines and oaks, and mountain (though not alpine) flora at heights of over 3,000ft together with a wide variety of birds of prey, while in some of the higher areas occurs a unique and fascinating series of relict plant communities termed by Knoche the 'Balearic zone': all this, it must be emphasised, within less than $12\frac{1}{2}$ miles (20km) radius from modern luxury hotels, a number of which now specialise in catering for the visiting naturalist.

Despite the recent popularity of the Balearics and Majorca in particular, it must not be thought that the islands are too commercialised, or are in any sense 'worked out' from the natural history viewpoint. Hundreds of ornithologists visit the islands every year, and additional information concerning migration through the area, distribution and numbers of regular species, and conditions governing the occurrence of vagrants is continually coming to light. The flora, mosses and ferns are fairly well known, but there is much scope for work on fungi in particular, and the insect communities have as yet been little explored while spiders appear to be virtually unknown. Fresh- and salt-water molluscs have likewise received little attention. There is consequently much to fascinate the amateur naturalist, while the specialist will find ample scope in fields such as insect and bird migration, and the development of insular races and varieties of various plant, insect and reptile species. In this latter respect, it is worth singling out the orchids and euphorbias as worthy of special study in the plant communities, and the endemic lizards and terrestrial molluscs as providing interesting examples of polymorphism.

Though these latter investigations may well prove beyond the resources of the amateur (and hence, strictly, the scope of this book), nevertheless the Majorcan fauna and flora provide such

Page 17 (above) Puig Major, from near Son March; (below) well-developed dune flora, with *Helichrysum stoechas*, *Echium arenarium*, spurges and occasional bushes of *Thymelaea hirsuta* in the foreground, and junipers and pines further back

Page 18 (*above*) The endemic sandwort *Arenaria balearica* growing on Puig Major; (*below*) an endemic member of the daisy family, *Bellium bellidioides*, at Cabo Formentor

scope for the study of the effects of insularity on plant and animal communities that it has been felt to justify the devotion of some space to this topic.

SCENERY AND CLIMATE

The island of Majorca owes much of its unique character to the great backbone mountain chain that rises abruptly out of the clear blue waters of the Mediterranean along its north-western coastline. The majestic peaks of this chain reach a climax in the massive bulk of Puig Major, which rears up to a height of 4,741ft (1,450m) near the centre of the range just to the north-east of Soller and less than 2½ miles (4km) inland. A good road winds up the mountainside from the small town of Soller, seeming to be heading straight for the heights of Puig Major before veering away to the right just below the peak and eventually tunnelling right through the main chain. From the entrance to the recently constructed tunnel, it is possible to look back down on to the minute streets and matchbox houses of Soller, nestling behind its little enclosed bay far below. Alternatively one can gaze out far across the valley to a tremendous vista of peaks stretching away to the south-west, or perhaps if one is lucky to watch a Bonelli's Eagle gliding fast along the thinly tree-clad slopes of these marvellous limestone crags so beloved of the delicate white *Cyclamen balearicum* which revels in their shady northern exposures and crevices. The final ascent from this tunnel to the nearby summit of Puig Major, well worth making for its even more spectacular views and for the botanical interest of the area, requires special permission, since it now supports a radar station—part of the American Early Warning System.

On through the tunnel, the road winds north-westwards through the Sierra de Torrellas and the scenically famous Gorg Blau. From Escorca, a few kilometres further on, it is possible during the summer months to take the four-hour walk down through the dried-up bed of the Torrent de Pareis between

B

walls towering up to over 900ft (300m), from which nesting crag martins continually wheel. The effect of these walls are such that some areas can be sweltering in a temperature of up to 104° F (40° C), while a little further on one finds oneself in almost complete darkness, with a considerable drop in temperature.

Further on, the road skirts the valley in which lies the Monastery of Lluch at a height of 1,300ft (400m), but securely sheltered by thick pinewoods, and then winds up between the peaks of Raig and Tomir, and finally by Ternellas, before dropping down by way of a series of rather hair-raising bends into the Bocquer Valley and thence to Pollensa. This north-eastern stretch harbours the main population of black vultures, as well as a number of other species of predators.

The mountain chain is of inestimable benefit to the economy of Majorca. In the first place, the superb scenery that it unfolds is in itself a great tourist attraction, but even more important, it provides an effective barrier against the ravages of the cold north wind that not infrequently (especially during the winter months) blasts down from the Continental landmass—in many cases no doubt the tail-end of the Mistral. As a result the lowland areas to the south-east enjoy even in midwinter a pleasantly mild climate, from which the relatively recently developed winter tourist trade is already benefiting enormously, while the islands' second major industry, agriculture, is a further benefactor.

The northern end of the chain offers perhaps the most spectacular scenic effects, the view from Mirador at the base of the Formentor Peninsula probably rivalling anything in Europe. Looking north-west, the successive vertical north-facing scarps of Pta de Sa Font Salada, Cap de Cataluna and Cabo Formentor jut out in steadfast opposition to the onslaught of the north wind, sheltering bays of pure transparent ultramarine, while to the west the sheer face of Pta de la Troneta rising vertically from the depths to over 800ft (250m) conjures up awesome thoughts of the tremendous orogenic (mountain-building) movements that led to its emergence.

Much of this northernmost area is virtually bare of vegetation in its more exposed areas, the woodland being confined to the southern slopes and the sheltered valleys such as Casas Veyas, which provide important gathering grounds for avian migrants in spring while they await the dropping of the northerly winds before renewing their journeying.

When the cold north wind blows, a thin mist often drifts in from the sea, above which the jagged peaks stand out in bas-relief until the gathering cloud banks gradually erase them from view, if not from memory. As the coming of spring brings greater warmth to the plains of the interior and the south-facing slopes, so the cloud base rises over the mountains until only the peaks are obscured. The condensation level then corresponds roughly to the upper limit of the tree line, and assumes marked significance as a limiting factor in the range of other plant communities at that altitude.

As one moves southwards along the mountains, mixed woodland appears more frequently on the exposed north-western slopes, while the more sheltered areas harbour olive groves and occasional orchards of citrus fruits. The maximum elevation of the tree line is reached in the Soller area, at about 3,000ft or 1,000m: thereafter the mountains drop gradually towards the south-west, terminating in the peninsula of Andraitx which shows a markedly more verdant aspect, being well wooded and extensively cultivated in spring. Almonds, figs and carobs are more frequent in this area, and the winter climate is distinctly milder. The contrast between the northern and southern extremities of the mountain chain, a mere 56 miles (90km) apart, is most marked and bears eloquent testimony to the effect of the north winds.

Condensation over the mountaintops, and the resulting precipitation which even in winter only very rarely takes the form of snow except on the extreme heights, is of importance in producing a supply of surface water early in the growing season. This is a great boon to the agricultural industry, for Majorca is singularly short of fresh water. The mountain torrents only flow intermittently following heavy rains during late autumn and early spring, and the water that they supply is used for irrigation while it lasts. A considerable amount of surface water is absorbed through the relatively permeable calcareous rocks that form the superstructure of the mountainous areas, re-appearing again at lower levels where the overlying sedimentary strata meet impermeable layers below. Thus, whereas the only mountain torrent to show any real permanence during the winter months is the Torrent de Pareis, the lower land of the central plain is served by a few small springs that maintain a fairly constant flow of water throughout the early part of the year. Even these, however, have almost entirely dried up by late April or May. Later in the season, many of the smallholdings rely on underground water supplies: this is particularly true in the south-east, where relatively recent sedimentary calcareous deposits overly deeper strata of impervious rocks. Water trick-ling down through the permeable layers has formed typical limestone grottoes, many of great size and spectacular beauty, which have been exploited as a tourist attraction. The best known are those of Hams and Drach—the latter extending for over 1½ miles (2km), and containing an elaborate amphitheatre where visitors can sit and listen to bands of musicians carried through the grottoes on illuminated boats.

Water from these underground supplies is raised in some cases by electrically driven pumps, but many of the smallholdings still rely on the age-old windmill, many of which can still be seen working in this south-eastern region, which is given over largely to dry farming, with a predominance of almonds and carobs, together with some vegetable crops. Much of the ground is too barren for cultivation, however, and varies from thin pinewoods through typical maquis vegetation to the very sparse garigue terrain so typical of the drier areas. Further north, a further magnificent series of grottoes, the Cuevas de Arta, stretch inland from the coast near Cañamel, containing many remarkable columnar stalactites, some reaching a height of over 65ft (20m), and considered to be amongst the most beautiful in the world. To the west, the Manacor, Lluchmayor, Felanitx area presents a more luscious appearance during the early months, indicative of a greater abundance of water, and this region is quite intensively farmed, vegetables and cereal crops appearing with greater frequency. Most of the farms keep livestock, particularly poultry and pigs: cattle are less frequently seen particularly during the summer months, since the peasant farmers believe that the intense glare of the sun harms their eyes, and consequently they are often only let out towards evening.

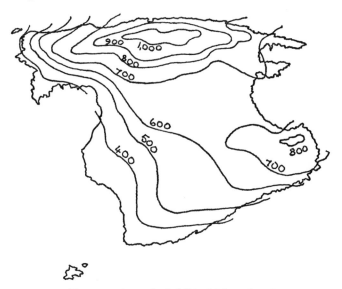

Figure 2   Annual rainfall in Majorca (mm)

Some isolated mountains of relatively minor elevation and more gentle contours occur in the generally hilly area of the south-central and south-east, including the peaks of Randa (1,800ft (548m)) and San Salvador (1,672ft (509m)), and culminating at their most easterly extension in the rather more impressive area around Arta, where Farruch and Morey rear up to 1,640ft (500m) and 1,828ft (560m) respectively. Only in this latter area do these mountains assume any climatic or biological significance, causing a slightly accentuated rainfall (Fig 2) and providing some cool, relatively damp north-facing crevasses and slopes that give restricted shelter to plant communities not unlike those found at much greater altitude in the 'Balearic zone' on Puig Major and its adjacent peaks.

Between the high Sierras of the north-west and these lower, scattered mountains of the east and south-east lies a beautifully sheltered stretch of central lowland, gently undulating and enjoying a sunny, almost subtropical climate. In winter the mid-day temperature averages rather over 50° F (10° C), ranging between 43° and 61° F (6° and 16° C), somewhat above the average for the western Mediterranean, and distinctly higher than the average for the north-west coast of the island, which is nearer 43° F (6° C). Snow is exceptional even in midwinter on this plain—it rarely descends below about 750m, and has only been recorded at sea level on some three or four occasions in the past ten years. The minimum temperature recorded at Palma over the same period is about 28·4° F (−2° C). Hail showers, at times associated with thundery weather, are rather more frequent, however, particularly in autumn, but fog and mist is fairly rare, being recorded at Palma on an average about five days per annum, though considerably more frequently along the north coast.

In summer, light sea breezes prevent the climate from becoming too torrid, and maintain a pleasantly hot 77° F (25° C), though temperatures as high as 96·8° F (36° C) have been recorded at times. Most days are clear and sunny, but the odd thunderstorm can occur, when brilliant displays of lightning play around the Sierras, and the occasional north wind can bring cloud drifting across from the higher peaks. The autumn rains generally begin towards the end of September, reaching a maximum during the following month, and rainfall remains fairly high up to the end of the year, thereafter decreasing quite rapidly.

The vegetation of this central plain varies markedly with the nature of the soil and the porosity of the underlying rock strata. Areas of almost bare calcareous rock supporting a thin garigue scrub alternate with pinewoods, olive groves, plantations of almond and fig trees, citrus fruit orchards, and numerous stretches of intensive cultivation on the richer soils. Windmills for tapping the underground water supply are again not infrequent.

Majorca supports three biologically important areas of mixed salt- and fresh-water marsh, namely those of Pto de Campos, the Albufera of Alcudia and the Albufereta of Pollensa. Campos also has a large stretch of still actively worked salt-pans, and a smaller area exists on the southern fringe of the Albufera. The relative salinity of these marshes varies from place to place and from season to season (according to the volume of fresh water draining into them from their surrounding catchment areas). As a consequence, they are able to support a wide variety of aquatic vegetation and insect life, which varies in abundance with the changing salinity. The large area of marshland in the Bay of Palma formerly known as El Prat has now been drained, and has virtually disappeared, but a further small area of marshland in the south-west near Magaluf has as yet been little studied, and could well repay closer investigation—it certainly supports a varied fauna of marsh birds and insects.

Turning now to the coastal scene, we find the north-west shoreline very barren and rocky (and also very inaccessible) with the exception of the almost entirely land-locked bay of Pto Soller, the small sandy cove at La Calobra—the mouth of the Torrent de Pareis, and the recently developed holiday resort of Cala de San Vicente in the north-east at the base of the Formentor Peninsula. This promontory gives shelter on its southern flank to some fine sandy beaches such as those at Formentor itself, while further more extensive stretches of sand occur in the Bahia de Pollensa and the Bahia de Alcudia, passing down the north-east coast, and along the 6 mile (10km) stretch of the shoreline of the Bahia de Palma at the opposite end of the island. The south-east coast is predominantly rocky, but boasts numerous little coves and inlets containing fine sandy bays, many of which are now blossoming into compact but flourishing holiday resorts.

Finally in this section mention must be made of the varied plant and animal associations that populate the extensive areas of sand dunes that lie behind the *playas*. These are particularly prominent in the Bay of Alcudia and along the east coast, and they used to be well developed in the bay of Palma before the coastal resorts sprang up all along the latter. Dunes in close proximity to one another may vary considerably in humidity, while some of the hollows lying near or below sea level receive salt-water seepage. Some of these dune associations are quite specialised, showing marked local variations, and are not at all typical of the rest of the littoral zone.

THE EFFECTS OF THE TOURIST TRADE

As a result of the equable, fresh climate, fine beaches and superbly varied scenery that it possesses, Majorca is now well established as an all-the-year-round holiday resort (although the winter tourist trade is of relatively recent growth and has not yet reached its full potential). Many holidaymakers now flock in to enjoy the Christmas and New Year hospitality, while a further wave arrives early in February when the island is garlanded in delicate almond-blossom. The main influx of spring visitors, including a large proportion of naturalists, occurs during April and May, coinciding with the main period of bird migration, and the peak of the flowering season (though some lowland species are past their best, while others of the mountains do not show to best advantage until June). Insects, both interesting and pestilential, are also showing their first climax of activity.

During the height of the summer season, planes carrying holidaymakers are arriving at Palma airport at a rate in the region of one every 2 minutes, and it is quite staggering to realise that the resident population of some 450,000 is outnumbered at least fourfold by the numbers of visitors that the island receives during the course of a single year, of whom well over a million are on holiday. Moreover, thanks to the impressive industry of the local construction workers, hotels and pensions are springing up at such a fantastic rate that during the 1960s visitors were being catered for at a rate that was showing an increase of some 14 per cent per annum, and the annual increase is still well in excess of 5 per cent.

Yet this is not to imply that Majorca is developing into a glorified holiday camp, for by and large the average holiday-maker is a gregarious animal, and by the construction of multistorey buildings skilfully blended into the background landscape (in some cases even built into recesses blasted out from the solid rock), the ever-increasing spate of visitors is being carefully channelled into a series of quite compact resorts. Though friendly and hospitable, the Majorcan is a keen businessman, and is quite well aware that the natural amenities of his island are in no small part responsible for the wealth of the tourist trade. Thus much of the countryside is being left quite unspoilt, so that within ten minutes' drive from the thriving capital of Palma with its modern waterfront hiding the true character of the busy city of narrow streets and open-air markets, it is possible to stop beside peasants tilling the fields with primitive tools beside their two-roomed smallholding with its ever-present windmill and perhaps a camel tethered by the door.

The only industrial development that is at present causing concern from the point of view of conserving natural amenities is the encroachment of building on the edge of the Albufera of Alcudia. In the 1860s a British company in fact attempted to drain the marsh, with the object of converting the reclaimed land to the cultivation of rice and cotton, but this project had to be abandoned though rice was eventually brought into cultivation on the verge of the marsh. Now there are proposals to renew the drainage operations, which, with the aid of modern equipment, will no doubt succeed. The idea behind the scheme is both to provide further land for building and agriculture, and at the same time restrict the breeding grounds of the hordes of mosquitoes that infest the marsh (and more particularly the salt-pans at its southern end). These can at times become pests in the nearby developing holiday resort of Ca'n Picafort during the height of the holiday season, particularly when the wind is in the west. The importance of conserving this marshland as a resting place for trans-Mediterranean migrant wading birds, and of the mosquito 'crop' as food for migrating flocks of swallows, martins and swifts will be enlarged upon later. Representations to this effect have already been made, but pressures from the construction industry will probably win this particular battle.

As yet the pinewoods along the shores and dunes of the Bay of Alcudia still remain, though building projects threaten these, too, and the resorts on the south-east coast may begin to spread before long, so there is evident need for active conservation measures to be undertaken in the immediate future if these important natural habitats are to be saved. It is encouraging that Max Nicholson has recently proposed at international level the creation of National Parks in the areas of Puig Major and the Formentor Peninsula. Even if the Albufera may eventually be lost, this proposal is at least a step in the right direction, and a much more feasible proposition.

CHAPTER TWO

A brief geological history

MUCH OF THE early geological history of the Balearic Isles—and of the western Mediterranean basin in general—is still a matter for active discussion, and any attempts to examine present trends of thought here would certainly be premature. In consequence, it is only proposed to outline the major geological events about which there is fairly good agreement, and to show how these have been responsible for giving rise to the present-day structure and relief of the islands, and what bearing they have on the animal and plant populations.

We can perhaps best appreciate the sequence of events from a starting point just following the end of the Carboniferous period, some 270 million years ago. About this time, restless movement of the vast land masses that now form Eurasia and Africa resulted in the great Hercynian orogeny, which elevated a series of mountain blocs in various parts of Europe. One of these was raised in what is now the western Mediterranean: though of relatively minor size and elevation it was to prove of great importance in the subsequent formation of the Balearics. There is some evidence to suggest that not long afterwards (in geological terms) renewed pressure by the northern land mass against this bloc threw up a ripple fold in a north-east/south-west direction, that now forms part of the underlying structure of the north-west Sierras of Majorca, notably in the Galatzo/Puig Major area.

During subsequent eras, the western Mediterranean region had a varied history, being successively raised and lowered on a number of occasions, as the water level of the incursive seas ebbed and flowed in response to the movement of the continental land masses. The exact details are still a matter of debate, but the point of principal interest to the present discussion is that several times during the next 150 million years the bloc that was to become the Balearics was variously joined to parts of both Eurasia and Africa by temporary land bridges. Thus the area received a variety of floral and faunal elements dating from different periods, that during spells of isolation or even resubmergence gradually or rapidly died off, to be replaced by new immigrant stock at each successive reopening of the land bridges. To follow such events in detail requires a very complete geological record, but unfortunately due to the various complexities introduced by erosion, faulting and other displacements, the evidence is rarely even adequate, let alone complete.

The earliest evidence for the existence of life in the Balearics comes from the occurrence of fossilised plant remains in rocks of the Devonian period, dating from about 400 million years ago, and plant fossils persist intermittently through to the Jurassic, during the next 250 million years, but the evidence is not sufficiently definite to permit association of Balearic life-forms with those of the adjacent continents until within the last 100 million years. Late in the Jurassic epoch, it seems likely that parts of Minorca were above the surface of the sea, but much of what is now Majorca was under extensive flood water, with the probable exception of the higher land of the north-west. Further elevation of Majorca took place in the Cretaceous, confirmed by the existence of globules of amber in the Gault Clay deposits laid down in the Upper Cretaceous, 90 million years ago, and found in some areas of the mountain foothills. Amber is the petrified resin exuded by trees, and points to the existence of extensive areas of afforestation on the emergent land during this period.

Some authorities believe that all the land of the Balearics was elevated by the end of the Cretaceous. By this time, a land bridge is also believed to have reunited the complex to Catalonia, but whether this was itself joined to the Eurasian mainland or formed a huge isolated landmass is rather less certain. It seems likely, however, that some present-day Majorcan life-forms could have their origins in colonisation that first took place at about this period.

Undoubtedly the most important event in the more recent geological history of Majorca was the series of extensive Alpine folding movements that occurred during the succeeding Eocene

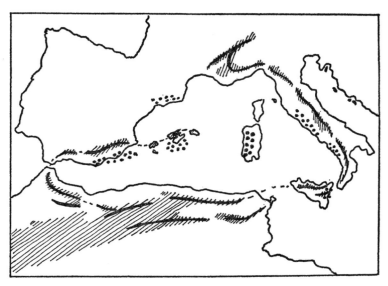

Figure 3   The Western Mediterranean Basin, showing the main trend lines of the Alpine folding movements together with volcanic blocs (dotted)

period about 70 million years ago. It is no exaggeration to say, in fact, that these massive earth movements have been largely responsible for the present physical form of much of southern Europe and North Africa. Originating in the Alps, one branch of this system travelled south, forming the backbone of Italy, and thence veered west through Sicily, reappearing in North Africa where it reached a climax in the Atlas range. Here further branching occurred, with one line of folding turning back northwards into the Iberian Peninsula and forming the Betic Cordillera in south-east Spain, from where it extended north-eastwards towards the Balearics. Looking at this orogenic movement with more particular reference to the Balearics, it becomes evident that pressure must have built up against the Hercynian bloc superimposing further folding on the original ripple fold, along the same north-east/south-west axis. Continuing pressure forced up a series of folds that eventually overlapped, accompanied by imbrication and faulting, producing the parallel ridges and surface sculpture in much the same form as it exists today. The direction of pressure can be well seen in the north-west Sierras of Majorca, and is reflected to a lesser extent in Ibiza. The scarp slopes face north-west, dropping straight into the sea, but along the gentler south-facing slopes a series of lakes developed as drainage water was trapped above the impermeable Jurassic layers. Alluvial deposits traceable to the late Eocene, some 50 million years ago, testify to the existence of these lakes.

The pattern of drainage in the western Mediterranean that was responsible for laying down the conglomerate coastline south-east of the Pyrénées during the Eocene strongly suggests that the Balearics and Catalonia formed a continuous elevated system at the time, and indeed fragments of granite and schists to be found along the coastlines (notably of Ibiza) show marked similarities to the crystalline massifs of Andalucia, in south-east Spain. Whether or not the actual linkage of the Balearics to the mainland occurred in the Cretaceous, or following the later Alpine movements (which in this area were probably of no great elevation in the initial stages), there is little doubt that a bridge with the mainland was firmly established by the lower Oligocene 40 million years ago. Evidence for this comes from the existence of fossilised mammalian remains in deposits laid down at this time in Majorca, that show marked similarity to those found in the Rhine valley, and in the vicinity of Languedoc.

Later in the Oligocene, some partial resubmergence must have occurred, involving at least the low-lying areas, since extensive Miocene deposits are to be found in central and south-eastern areas of Majorca. By the Upper Miocene, during the last 18 million years, a further cycle of elevation began, raising the

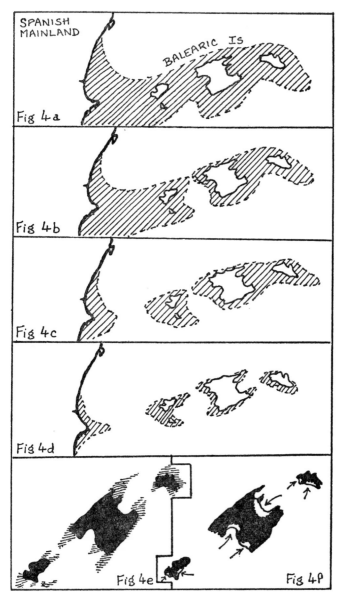

Figure 4 Geological development of the Balearic Islands (modified from Colom): a Upper Miocene—12 million years; b Upper Pliocene—1 million years; c and d progressive stages of submergence early in the Quaternary; e later in the Quaternary—200,000 years; f the laying down of the Tyrrhenian beaches, completed by 30,000 years

mountain chain to approximately its present elevation, but thereafter the fate of the peninsula becomes rather uncertain again. Some authorities believe that it remained joined to Catalonia, but others hold that reunion with the Continent may not have been effected until much later. Scharff has deduced from the evidence of fossil molluscs that the Islands were still joined to Andalucia in the Pliocene, but there could well have been intermediate rupture of the land bridge.

However this may be, there now seems to be general agreement that at some time towards the Upper Pliocene about a million years ago, the bridge of relatively low land between Ibiza and Majorca was finally broken for the last time, isolating the Majorca/Minorca complex from the mainland of Catalonia. Very early in the Quaternary era, 800,000 years ago, Ibiza/ Formentera in turn suffered rupture as a separate unit, and by about 500,000 years ago further submergence had separated Majorca from Minorca. By the late Quaternary, it seems likely that the individual islands first assumed their present form, though the region was by no means stabilised.

Continuing gradual submergence eventually inundated the whole central plain and much of the southern part of the Majorcan mainland, though the south-east coast remained above the surface. Final re-emergence occurred in the Pleistocene, and during the Great (Mindel-Riss) Interglacial warm period, the final development of the laying down of the ecologically important Tyrrhenian beaches in the bays of Palma and Alcudia, and at Campos took place, some 30,000 years ago.

PRESENT STRUCTURE

In the Sierras, we find the surface layers of rock composed of deep-sea calcareous deposits originating for the most part during the Miocene, with the possible exception of the higher peaks. The extensive folding and rupturing that took place towards the end of this period, followed by subsequent erosion along the more permanent watercourses has exposed Jurassic strata, which

Page 35 (*above*) The garigue, with *Asphodelus microcarpus* in the background and *Sonchus spinosus* on the left and *Astragalus poterium* nearer the camera; (*below*) a fine clump of *Helichrysum stoechas* on the dunes

Page 36 Two very similar spiny plants of the garigue; (*above*) *Anthyllis fulgurans*; (*below*) *Sonchus spinosus*

also appears in areas of faulting. These underlying rocks of a partially dolomitic nature are distinctly dense and durable, in contrast to the surface layers which in some areas have been weathered to fine pinnacles by rainwater. Fissures resulting from the folding also allow the penetration of Triassic rocks in a number of areas, showing close affinity with those of the French Alps in particular. Outcrops of gypsum are not uncommon in the Sierras, and may assume some local ecological significance with respect to plant growth.

The valley bottoms have suffered considerable surface erosion, revealing reddish layers of primarily volcanic origin and rich mineral content, accounting for their extraordinary fertility. Alluvial deposits lie along the base of the southern flanks of the Sierras, dating from the Upper Eocene, and consist of fertile marls interspersed with lignite deposits that have been extensively mined. Knoche has described a variety of fossilised plant remains from these deposits that are very similar to those occurring in the vicinity of Aix-en-Provence. Of much more recent (Quaternary) origin, are series of mollusc beds to be found principally in the north-east and south of the island.

The Sierras de Levante in the eastern region form a less regular series of folds believed to be of rather more recent origin than the main peaks of the north-west. They consist in the main of Triassic and Jurassic strata overlaid by essentially calcareous deposits of the Lower Cretaceous or the characteristically grey Miocene deposits. Large areas of the south-eastern lowlands are covered by block deposits of various thickness dating from the late Miocene or early Quaternary; they are very similar to those forming much of the relatively flat surface of Minorca. The Quaternary deposits of the south and east coasts consist largely of rather friable and porous rock, and consequently support a flora more essentially adapted to drier conditions.

Miocene deposits occur largely on the central plain, later overlaid by Quaternary alluvial beds, which suffered variable erosion according to the underlying structure that had been developed during the Tertiary. As this took the form of a

C

gentle rippling along the main north-east/south-west axis of
folding, reflecting the main pressure thrusts of the Alpine movement, the underlying layers thrust through the alluvial deposits as
a series of low hills running parallel to the main axis of the Sierras.
Otherwise, Miocene littoral deposits alternate with beds laid
down in the Oligocene throughout much of the north-central
area. The result is to produce an alternation of rather bare areas
of thin soil coverage, with a series of distinctly fertile troughs
that have been intensively cultivated.

CHAPTER THREE

Flowering plants

THE FLORA OF the Mediterranean region as a whole is character-ised by a wealth of variety and a general abundance that can be rivalled by very few areas of comparable size anywhere in the world, and within this area the island of Majorca is able to lay claim to rather more than its fair share of attractive and unusual flowers. Nevertheless, it is sad to have to record that man, by persistent over-exploitation has done, and is still doing his best to erase much of the natural beauty of form and colour that once delighted the eye. Hillsides that were once forest-covered and lush with floriferous growth have been laid bare, leaving stark exposures of rock but thinly covered by tufts of coarse grasses and a few spiny shrubs. Even on the fertile lowland plains where a richer soil covering has accumulated, the flora is being radically altered by the use of weedkillers, drainage of the marshes, and other measures designed to improve the land for agriculture or building.

Fortunately, however, the plight of the island in these respects is rather less severe than that of many areas of the Mediterranean coastline. This is largely due to its more maritime climate and the considerable elevation of the mountain chain which results in a relatively high rainfall along the north-west coast during spring and again in autumn, permitting rather longer growing seasons than is usual on the mainland, and allowing moisture-loving plants to survive in sufficiently humid areas. It is possibly also connected with the fact that many early adventurers seeking to colonise the western Mediterranean from the ancient civilisa-tions of the east tended to bypass Majorca because of its relative lack of mineral wealth. Archaeological evidence suggests that man did not actively colonise Majorca and the other Balearic islands until about 2,000 BC or possibly later, whereas in the 6th millennium BC Neolithic culture had already spread into the Iberian Peninsula, and even reached Britain as early as 2,500 BC. What this amounts to, is to suggest that the human race has so far had rather less opportunity to desecrate the natural beauty of the island than has been the case in other less fortunate countries. As it seems that Majorca is now beginning to attract the attention of conservationists, let us hope that a more enlightened outlook will save the wealth of plant life that still exists on the island at the present time.

SCOPE OF MAJORCAN FLORA

The scope of Majorcan flora is remarkable, considering the small dimensions of the island. It combines elements of the primeval Mediterranean forests, typical maquis and garigue associations characteristic of arid areas where the rainfall is low and the underlying limestone rock highly porous, sub-alpine plants of the higher peaks, rich Mediterranean flora of the fertile valley floors, sandy pinewoods carpeted with an infinite variety of orchids, characteristic specialist associations of sand dunes, salt marshes and sea cliffs, and finally a unique 'Balearic zone' that contains rare and fascinating plants.

In the early 1920s, Knoche, in the most recent comprehensive survey of the flora of the Balearic Islands recorded some 1,300 flowering plants (including the grasses and sedges), a truly staggering total, and of these all but a very small minority were to be found within the confines of Majorca itself. The list includes over 40 endemic species, and a further 20 or so distinct local varieties that warrant at least subspecific status. Some idea of the variety that this implies can be gained when one realises that the list is not very far short of the total for the whole of the British Isles—an area very nearly 100 times as large as that occupied by the Balearic complex.

During the last half-century, it is probable that some (though fortunately not many) of these plants will have disappeared—though there is always the possibility of rediscovering in some of the more remote and as yet relatively unexplored mountainous areas one of the endemics now believed to be extinct.

However, if some species have been lost, it is equally true that other plants previously unknown or unrecognised have been more recently discovered. Some have been artificially introduced, while others are in the process of gradual progressive change. For the components of an island community such as this are never static: relict species eventually give up the fight for survival as the habitat to which they have become adapted through more and more specialised evolutionary modifications gradually disappears, but other more vigorous species with greater potential for variation begin a process of active evolution. Chance mutations throw up new varieties that appreciate the changing conditions, and thrive in the modified habitats that are continually being produced by the activities of man.

Among the group of relict species, it is possible to distinguish two distinct types. On the one hand we have plants such as the myrtle (*Myrtus communis*) and the carob (*Ceratonia siliqua*), which though still quite well represented in Majorca, and widespread throughout much of the rest of the Mediterranean basin, can be regarded as of relict status in that they represent the sole surviving species of families that in prehistoric times were believed to form an integral part of the plant life of the region. By contrast, we find in the presence on the island of the rue-leaved saxifrage *Saxifraga tridactylites*, *S. corsica* (a close relative of the meadow saxifrage *S. granulata*), and *Primula acaulis alba* (an endemic white primrose), three plants that are the sole representatives remaining in the Balearics of genera that are elsewhere widespread throughout Europe—suggesting that in former times a more humid climate prevailed. The former is confined to shady rock faces, while the latter occupies only three known sites in shady, humid rifts on rocky peaks (and may now be extinct in one or two of these sites). There seems little doubt from this and other evidence that at one time, probably towards the end of the successive Ice Ages, Majorca once supported a quite extensive alpine flora.

In direct contrast to these survivors of bygone ages, the orchids, vetches, spurges and members of the *Compositae* (daisy family) are present in bewildering profusion and variety. Within these groups, it is quite common to find evidence of interbreeding and local modification that are a sure indication of plants in a progressive state of evolution. These are at once a source of intense interest but perpetual confusion in the botanical world (and perhaps of potential suicide to the enthusiastic amateur?) though at least showing that not all living things are threatened by the changes that come in the wake of expanding human civilisation.

Between these two evolutionary extremes occur a variety of relatively stable plant communities which, though each possessing their own special characteristics, conform in general structure to a number of well-defined Mediterranean types. In this climatic region, the optimum form of vegetative development is seen in the evergreen forest, which in prehistoric times used to clothe the shores and hillsides of virtually all the Mediterranean countries. A special feature of this forestland was the ability of the trees that it contained to withstand a period of extensive summer drought, and we find that they essentially comprise two groups—the pines, in which the leaves are reduced to cylindrical grooved needles, and the oaks which have thick, leathery leaves covered with a waxy coating, both characteristics of use in cutting down moisture loss by transpiration during the long, hot summers.

With the advent of man, the thinning out of the forests began, the oaks in particular providing hard resistant timber excellent for constructional purposes. Natural regeneration was prevented by the introduction of close-grazing sheep and browsing goats, while other surviving seedlings were choked by the coarse clumps of *Ampelodesmus* grass that invaded the clearings. Desiccation and erosion of the topsoil quickly followed, and in a relatively short time the forest could degenerate through a more or less clearly defined series of intermediate stages to the arid, stony grassland or steppe that characterises many coastal stretches around the Mediterranean. The steppe vegetation consists largely of a few precocious but colourful annuals that can complete their life cycles during the brief rainy seasons of spring and autumn, together with a variety of perennial species that can survive the summer heat in the form of underground storage organs after the food-producing green parts have been scorched and withered in the fierce sun.

Two important intermediate stages can be recognised in this degenerative process. These comprise the *maquis* vegetation which consists of a layer of taller shrubs and small trees usually in the range 3–12ft (1–4m) high, and the *garigue*, an arid association of sub-shrubs often protected from the attentions of grazing animals by the possession of spiny leaves or branchelets interspersed with the coarse steppe grasses, which can combine to shelter a variety of interesting herbaceous plants. Though Majorca contains representative patches of all these types of vegetation, the unusual variation in climate, physical features and soil porosity that exists between different areas has resulted in much intergrading and local differentiation. As a result, it is only the evergreen forest and the taller (or primary) maquis that can be regarded as to any real extent cosmopolitan, while the low maquis and garigue shows such distinctive variation between different areas that each situation requires individual treatment.

This is doubly true when it is realised that it is in the very areas where the overlap of the different vegetative types occurs that many of the most interesting plant associations are to be found. It is here where species characteristic of the different communities come into conflict and competition, that the dramas of evolution are continually being enacted before our eyes: it is here that we can see relict species struggling to survive, while alongside them new, evolving forms struggle even more vigorously to ensure their birthright. Coming further and further down the degenerative slope from the climax forest vegetation, we find that particular local influences exert a more marked effect, and more and more endemic species make their appearance in more and more specialised habitats. This is particularly true in the case of the mountain flora, where many of the endemic species are concentrated in a narrow zone just below the normal cloudbase, but rather above the level to which the more typically 'Mediterranean' flora aspires. Knoche has named this the 'Balearic zone', and the extent to which local variations in climate can influence this zone is shown by the fact that it varies in altitude from about 3,300ft (900–1,100m) in the central Sierras down to about 1,300ft (300–500m) in the north-east of the island, only some 25 miles (40km) away, and typically descends a good 650ft (200m) lower on the cool, steep, north-west facing scarps than it does on the rather gentler sunny southern slopes. Its altitude is roughly indicated in the north-east by the presence of the palmeto (*Chamaerops humilis*), and more will be said about the many unique plants that it shelters at a later stage, but this detail must be painted in against a background of the vegetation more typical of the main associations already mentioned.

THE EVERGREEN FORESTS

The remnants of the Majorcan forests consist in the main of two quite distinct types of woodland—the thin, open stands of Aleppo pine (*Pinus halipensis*), and the more dense coverage provided by the expanses of holm oak (*Quercus ilex*) that clothe the mountain slopes. The distribution of the latter is closely related to the areas of maximum precipitation, as the woods are essentially confined to an area near the base of the Arta Peninsula, and otherwise to the heights of the north-western Sierras, where they appear predominantly on the north-facing exposures. The pines, however, show a much more catholic distribution, and occur in a variety of sites throughout the island, albeit more typically on the sand dunes of the littoral zone, and the less shady slopes of the Sierras: perhaps the most extensive stands are found on the Andraitx Peninsula, in the south-west.

Both species extend to the upper limit of the tree zone, at about 3,775–3,940ft (1,150–1,200m).

Knoche makes the point that towards the upper limit of this zone, the oak trees invade the pinewoods more frequently than vice versa, and he suggests that this may be an indication that the pines are of more recent origin. While this may be true, it seems more likely that following thinning of both types of woodland, the more spreading habit of the oak would be more likely to prevent infiltration by the pines.

Even in the height of summer, the dense canopy of the oak-woods preserves a dark, relatively humid atmosphere that restricts the development of much in the way of undergrowth. Ferns and mosses are plentiful, and ivy occurs here and there, but these apart there only remain a few intrusive shrubs from the maquis vegetation, together with a select group of shade-loving species, among which the delicate white-flowered *Cyclamen balearicum* takes pride of place. In the open, this slender-

Figure 5   Distribution of the Aleppo pine *Pinus halipensis*, shaded, and the holm oak *Quercus ilex*, in black (after Colom)

petalled cyclamen flourishes in deep crevices in the limestone
rocks, where the corms are often buried a foot or more deep
in the rubble which provides the good drainage yet cool root-
run that these plants need. Through this debris, long stems
struggle upwards to the light, but among the cool shade of the
oaks the corms often lie just beneath the surface, and the leaves
and flowers form a much more compact clump, in which the
true character of the plant can better be appreciated. Other
denizens of the undergrowth include the ever-present trailing
thorny stems of *Smilax aspera*, and occasional plants of virgin's
bower (*Clematis cirrhosa*) which may climb 10–13ft (3–4m)
through the foliage to meet the sun—as does the curious honeysuckle *Lonicera implexa*, in which the upper leaves are often fused
together around the stem. Here and there the Mediterranean
heath (*Erica multiflora*) blooms in patches of deeper soil, but it
does not appreciate too much shade.

The thinner stands of pine occupy in the main rather drier
sites, and the more open, sunny atmosphere promotes a more
extensive and varied shrub layer in which many of the typical
plants of the maquis occur, including rosemary (*Rosmarinus
officinalis*), rock roses (*Cistus* spp), sun roses (*Helianthemum* spp),
the lentisk (*Pistacia lentiscus*), asphodels and brooms, while the
heaths *Erica arborea* and *E. multiflora* are plentiful in the more
humid areas. Probably the greatest fascination that these woodland glades will provide for the visiting botanist, however, will
come from the orchids. Though more typical of the stony
garigue, the porous, well-drained yet moisture-retentive sandy
soil of the pinewoods seems to suit them well, and they can be
found scattered around clearings in bewildering variety, their
delicate colouring often contrasting vividly with the brilliant
background of scarlet and blue provided by the pimpernels
(*Anagallis arvensis* forms) that cover much of the ground with
trailing carpets during their spring flowering season.

The Venus orchid (*Ophrys speculum*), the ubiquitous *O. fusca*,
the low-growing, stocky bumble bee orchid (*O. bombyliflora*)
and the delightful sawfly orchid (*O. tenthredinifera*) with broad,

delicate greenish-pink sepals can be found with a little patience, while the more diligent searcher will be rewarded by less frequent patches of the even more beautiful *O. bertolonii*, with its dark hairy lip and narrow, deep pink wings. All these insect orchids hybridise freely, often throwing up distinctive local varieties, and some particularly attractive forms occur notably in the south-east suggestive of an *O. tenthredinifera* × *O. bertolonii* parentage. They all prefer a high lime content in the soil, and in areas where the limestone rocks are close to the surface, scattered clumps of the man orchid (*Aceras anthropophorum*) occur, sometimes to be found growing on almost bare rock. The tongue orchids (*Serapias* spp) prefer the drier areas of thin pinewoods in the south and south-west of the island, and indeed a good selection of orchids can be found within easy walking distance of the centre of Palma, in the grounds of the Castello de Bellver on the hilltop to the west of the city.

Pinewoods on more stony ground support spiny shrubs of the lower maquis, including more compact plants of *Smilax aspera*, butcher's broom (*Ruscus aculeatus*) and the *Asparagus* spp—all closely related—while among crevices in the more open areas the endemic cyclamen is joined by the yellow-spathed *Arum italicum* and the quaint friar's cowl (*Arisarum vulgare*). It is one of the many surprises of the Majorcan flora to find this and the Mediterranean heath, both for long believed to be lime-haters, flourishing in soil with a calcium content of about 30 per cent! All these plants (except the heath), together with numerous of the smaller spurges (*Euphorbia* spp) are equally at home on similar stony ground in the olive groves, and shelter a number of annual vetches which can provide quite a colourful carpet in spring.

Finally in this section, brief reference must be made to the other trees that occur on the island. A few stands of stone pine (*Pinus pinea*) are to be found, mainly in lowland areas, but all have the appearance of having been planted, though the kermes oak (*Quercus coccifera*) which occurs among the primary maquis of the south-west and in the mountain foothills may well be native. Relics of bygone eras include the maple (*Acer opalus*), once very widespread in the forests, but now confined to the more humid, inaccessible gorges of the Sierras, and the endemic box (*Buxus balearicus*) which still survives in shady valleys. This latter species was also quite plentiful in former times, but was extensively exploited for carving, and also for its attractive fresh perfume.

This plant association comprises the taller shrubs that attain a height of about 7–16ft (2–5m), and is dominated in Majorca by the lentisk (*Pistacia lentiscus*). When flowering in spring, the catkins of this bush give off clouds of reddish pollen which can virtually smother anyone pushing his way through it. Being a hay-fever sufferer of long standing, I expected this to affect me badly, but it turned out for me at least, to be perfectly harmless. Besides providing the valuable resin, gum mastic, so widely used in medicine and in the manufacture of varnishes, the black berries form the basis of a liqueur known as *mastiche* that used to be very popular particularly in countries around the eastern basin of the Mediterranean.

The other trees and shrubs associated with the lentisk include the olive (*Olea europa*) and (though much more thinly distributed) the carob. Both are, of course, extensively cropped, olives and olive oil being one of the principal exports of the Balearics though rather less important in world markets now than in former days, while the carob provides the locust beans, a valuable fodder crop, and even used to supplement human diet in times of food shortage.

The tall shrub *Phillyrea angustifolia*, close relative of the olive, and the smaller *Daphne gnidium* are well distributed in most areas of maquis, but the strawberry tree (*Arbutus unedo*) tends to prefer shady areas on the mountain slopes and lower ground, where it often associates with myrtle and the tree heath. The dark-berried juniper (*Juniperus oxycedrus*) occurs with myrtle in the damp valleys of the Sierras, where it reaches an elevation of

3,000ft, but otherwise is only found among the damper areas of the dunes of the Bay of Alcudia, the red-berried Phoenician juniper (*J. phoenicea*) replacing it elsewhere in the lowland maquis.

Primary maquis associations of this kind occur over much of the island, but usually in relatively small patches, and only reach extensive proportions in the foothills of the Sierras, where they intergrade with the evergreen forest, and along the east coast. At its best, the taller maquis can become almost impenetrable, leaving little scope for undergrowth, though the ubiquitous *Smilax aspera*, spiny *Asparagus* spp, and madder (*Rubia peregrina*) combine effectively to seal the odd gaps.

SECONDARY MAQUIS AND LOWLAND GARIGUE

The dominant plants of the lower maquis vary according to location. In the north-east rosemary (*Rosmarinus officinalis*), palmeto and the tall fronds of the elegant but coarse grass *Ampelodesmus mauritanicus* strive for control, interspersed with the beautiful endemic member of the St John's wort family, *Hypericum balearicum* which appears to be comfortably holding its own. Moving south-west through the mountains, the area around the Ternellas valley supports a vigorous association of the bright yellow thorny broom (*Calycotome infesta*), which makes a brilliant show in May and June, the large Mediterranean spurge (*Euphorbia characias*), and the dazzling white flowers of the rock rose (*Cistus monspeliensis*) set off beautifully by the narrow, rather glossy dark green leaves, interspersed here and there in the more humid areas with the Mediterranean heath. This white rock-rose is co-dominant with *Cistus albidus*, which sports much larger pink tissue-paper petals against paler olive-green foliage, throughout the cistus scrub of most of the rest of the island interspersed with rosemary and the prickly shrubs *Asparagus albus* and *A. stipularis*. The rosemary of the lowland maquis is, however, but a poor counterpart of the mountain form. Plants of the plains vary from a pale washed-out blue to a faded

pinkish lavender, whereas on the northern exposures of the
Formentor Peninsula in particular, some very fine plants occur,
with flowers of a pure deep luminous blue.

Lavender (*Lavendula dentata*) is virtually restricted to the
south-west of the island, as is the rather local rock rose *Cistus
clusii*, which latter is replaced towards the north-east by the sage-
leaved rock rose (*Cistus salvaefolius*) which requires deeper,
richer soil. Before leaving the *Cistus* spp, mention must be made
of the curious plant *Cytinus hypocistis* which has no green parts
at all, being entirely parasitic on the roots of the various rock
roses. In its best varieties, the globular yellow flower heads
surrounded by bright red fleshy bracts look for all the world
like small fancy cream cakes covered with icing, planted in the
bare soil. These weird plants are known from the south of the
island near Cabo de Salinas, and probably occur elsewhere in
view of the general distribution of the host plants, but not all
forms are as conspicuous as that described here.

Other families that show a discontinuous distribution throughout the island include the sun roses (*Helianthemum* spp), the
characteristic *H. fumana* that occurs at moderate elevations
throughout much of the Sierras being replaced in the south by
a variety of species including *H. laevipes*, *H. origanifolium* and
H. caput-felis and others, some of quite restricted, local distribution. The brooms also show interesting distributional quirks, for
whereas *Calycotome infesta* is widespread in much of the central
and northern maquis, it is replaced in the south and east by the
rather paler, endemic *Genista lucida*, the range of the two over-
lapping in the region of the Arta Peninsula. The very floriferous
Genista cinerea prefers the sun-facing slopes of the Sierras,
where its graceful arching branches show to best effect, while
the much rarer Spanish broom (*Spartium junceum*) frequents
similar situations.

Turning now to the drier areas of lowland scrub maquis, where
the vegetation approaches true garigue, we find at every turn
the plant that truly lays claim to expressing the character of
Majorcan vegetation. Everywhere on barren wasteland from

mountain top to coastal sand dune, from most inhospitable
vertical cliff face to friendly meandering country roadside can
be found blooming the tall white spires of the asphodel (*Asphodelus microcarpus*), though how any aspect of this plant could be
described as *micro* defeats the imagination, for in well-developed
clumps the starry spikes may reach to a height of 7ft (2m) or
more, while the lance-shaped leaves can spread to well over 3ft
(1m).

This species provides a useful indication of the extent of variation in the climate found in the different parts of the island. On
the south-west coast, it is typically in flower by the end of
February, whereas most plants of the central plain are not in
bloom until late March or early April, and those of the high
Sierras may not flower until June. Excursions to Puig Major
have reported the first plants just opening from bud on the peak
itself in the first week of July.

The smaller *A. albus* is scattered thinly, mainly in the mountains, while the more delicate *A. fistulosus* prefers the drier
south-western parts of the island. In this lowland garigue is the
true home of the spiny shrubs *Asparagus albus* and *A. stipularis*,
madder, a bewildering variety of spurges, and the strong-
smelling rue (*Ruta chalepensis*). These shelter a variety of short-
lived annual herbs, and numerous bulbous species which include
the wild garlics *Allium rotundum*, *A. roseum* (the familiar rose
garlic) and more rarely *A. subhirsutum*—the latter more typically
a plant of the mountain slopes—the tassel hyacinth (*Muscari
comosum*), an endemic form of *Crocus minimus*, and the pale blue
Iris sisyrinchium, the flowers of which may only last a single day.
In coastal areas, they are joined by the sea squill (*Urginea maritima*), which does not flower until autumn: this is a rather
disappointing plant, with its clustered spike of white flowers
looking like a congested asphodel, belying the promise of the
enormous bulbs that may be as large as a grapefruit.

The rocky hillsides hold numerous small orchids, together
with the taller, pink-flowered *Orchis italica*, and the wall penny-
wort (*Umbilicus rupestris*), while sunny slopes in the north-east

in particular are covered with the tree spurge (*Euphorbia den-droides*), which in favourable situations can attain a height of up to 7ft (2m), and can provide welcome splashes of colour on otherwise bare hillsides. Annuals in this habitat include a num-ber of vetches, and several interesting and colourful varieties of restharrows (*Ononis* spp), and clovers (*Trifolium* spp), not for-getting the smaller spurges which are so confusing for the amateur.

GARIGUE AND STEPPE VEGETATION OF THE FORMENTOR PENINSULA

This is perhaps the most interesting area for the visiting botanist —particularly if he is restricted to a short stay—in that it com-bines ease of access by means of a well-surfaced if rather hazar-dous road with a good cross-section of the endemic flora. Clumps of *Genista cinerea* and *Calycotome infesta* clothe the valleys in brilliant yellow during May and June, interspersed with the pale mauve *Erica multiflora*, but these soon give way to typical palmeto/*Ampelodesmus* scrub as the road winds its way up out of the valleys towards a series of viewpoints giving breathtaking vistas out over the north-facing sea cliffs. Soon by the roadside appears the first of the endemics, the beautiful *Hypericum baleari-cum*, which prefers sheltered, sunny exposures, and is hardly ever without its starry yellow flowers. It does, however, come into full bloom in late spring, when the bushes are covered in deep yellow, contrasting vividly with the small, curiously crinkled leaves of an attractive shade of deep green. At slightly higher elevations, the first of the true garigue vegetation is encountered, and continues intermittently on the higher peaks right to the northernmost tip of Cap Formentor. The large stumps of asphodel, and clumps of coarse grasses dominate the flatter areas, wherever sufficient soil has been able to accumulate, but between these nestle an intriguing variety of little 'hedgehogs', ground-hugging, bun-shaped spiny plants that seem to be glued to the very rock face.

The deeper green, more distinctly domed cushions belong to

Page 53 (left) *Pastinaca lucida*;
(below) the foxglove
Digitalis dubia

Page 54 (left) Pitch trefoil
Psoralea bituminosa;
(below) large yellow
restharrow Ononis natrix

another endemic plant, *Astragalus poterium*, and close inspection will reveal the vetch-like leaves set among the spiny branches. Towards the end of April and during May these hummocks can become literally covered with the small, pale mauve winged flowers so characteristic of the milk-vetches. Closely associated, and apparently in vigorous competition with this species is the much greyer germander *Teucrium subspinosum*, which, as with the rosemary, exists in a variety of colour forms. The *Astragalus/Teucrium* associations are a dominant feature of large areas of mountain garigue throughout Majorca, but reach their lower exposures on the Formentor Peninsula, the former often descending to sea level in the gullies, where the seed is carried by temporary torrents during the rainy seasons.

Two other spiny shrubs in close competition with the foregoing may at first sight appear quite grey and dead during the early spring months, but at close range one reveals narrow trifoliate leaflets at the intersections of the branches, while the other appears to have some kind of hawkweed growing beneath it. Return visits in June will disclose both species in flower—the former covered in minute whitish-mauve flowers of a vaguely pea-like character that betray its identity as *Anthyllis fulgurans*, but the latter sporting quite large typical yellow *Hieracium* flowers springing directly from angles of the thick, woody stems. This latter plant is *Sonchus spinosus*, and it occurs not just in the mountain garigue but also on rocks at the seashore, particularly at the base of the Arta Peninsula. Alongside it in the garigue occurs *Smilax aspera balearica*, a very congested, close-growing form of this usually trailing plant, and even more surprising are occasional plants of lentisk growing in slight hollows of deeper soil, but spreading horizontally and hugging the ground, reaching less than 20in ($\frac{1}{2}$m) in height.

These spiny and close-growing species resist the attention of the goats that roam freely over the whole peninsula, and shelter other interesting species, including a number of small leguminous plants of the genera *Medicago* and *Ononis*, the small bulbous *Romulea parviflora* and the tissue-paper bracts of *Paronychia*

D

Figure 6   1 *Sonchus spinosus*; 2 *Romulea parviflora*; 3 *Paronychia argentea*; 4 *Hippocrepis balearica*;   5 *Astragalus poterium*;   6 *Anthyllis fulgurans*; 7 *Teucrium subspinosum*; 8 *Teucrium polium*; 9 *Smilax aspera balearica*

argentea, while long stems of the pink-flowered milkwort *Polygala rupestris* straggle among the rocks, and more surprising still, the trailing tendrils of the parasitic *Cuscuta planiflora* creep across the ground from host to host.

When visiting this area, the tourist should not neglect the sheer north-facing cliffs. Here hang trails of the bright blue-flowered form of rosemary, together with patches of the large silver-grey felted leaves of the endemic 'everlasting' *Helichrysum lamarckii* which towards midsummer on these northerly exposures become covered with yellow powder-puff flowers. Everywhere in the rocks appear a variety of *Compositae* including the curious relative of the hawkweeds *Hyoseris radiata*, the leaves of which are deeply cut into triangular lobes, giving them an ivy-like appearance.

Moving on through the valley past Casas Veyas, well-known resting and gathering place for migrant birds, towards the tip of the peninsula, the road passes through a tunnel and here moisture lingers even through the height of summer, supporting an interesting flora including the endemic *Erodium chamaedryoides*, a valuable rock-garden plant in view of its long flowering season, and other even more attractive (but less permanent) storksbills, while here and there in less accessible areas flourish clumps of the beautiful carmine-pink paeony (*Paeonia cambessedesii*). On the southerly exposures of these same cliffs can be found occasional clumps of switch-like branches of the rather rare joint-pine (*Ephedra fragilis*), while the stony, tree-clad gullies shelter cyclamen, friar's cowl and the arums *Arum italicum* and *A. muscivorum*. In this area, it is disconcerting to find the endemic 'hedgehogs', including some of the world's rarest plants, actually growing in the tarmac on the verges of the roads!

Near the Cap itself grow a number of species more typical of the sea cliffs, including the rare endemic groundsel *Senecio rodriguezii*, and various sea lavenders (*Statice* spp) which are difficult to classify as they grow in a number of different forms according to situation, but are none the less attractive, forming tight grey-green almost succulent-looking mounds on the bare rock face, covered by slender jointed stems of small flowerheads in varying shades of purple or pink. The papery *Paronychia* is encountered again, together with the small eidelweiss-like *Evax pygmaea*, and on every surface or crevice that carries any vestige of soil, the lovely little purple daisy *Bellium bellidoides* flowers its head off throughout the spring, and often again in the autumn. Finally, in some of the lower gullies approaching sea level occurs an endemic buckthorn *Rhamnus ludovici salvatoris*, which is quite distinct from other Mediterranean forms (not to be confused with the polymorphic *R. oleoides* which occurs in the same area) and was made much of by Knoche, since he detected in it a strong resemblance to *R. croceus*, which occupies similar latitudes in California, and may consequently have evolved in similar fashion.

GARIGUE OF THE ARTA MOUNTAINS

Broadly speaking, this area bears many similarities to the associations of the Formentor Peninsula, but it has a number of individual features that make it well worth a visit—if only for the fact that a minor but quite good road from Arta (difficult to find, but signposted to the Ermita de Betlen) passes right over the crest of the mountains, rendering access exceptionally easy, and the view from some of these peaks is magnificent.

Considering how exposed the tops are, it is surprising how much *Hypericum balearicum* they harbour, together with the usual asphodel and palmeto, interspersed with the typical dominant 'hedgehogs', *Astragalus poterium* and *Teucrium subspinosum*, which as usual shelter a variety of herbaceous species, notably of the pea family, together with small, thyme-like *Micromeria* spp.

The north-facing scarps, however, provide a much more interesting and surprisingly varied flora. The large, felted grey leaves of *Helichrysum lamarckii* are fairly plentiful, as are hawkweeds in variety, but the most beautiful plant without doubt is a particularly fine colour form of *Coris monspeliensis*, a heath-like, usually biennial plant, with rather large tubular flowers of a brilliant mauve. Were it not so short-lived, this would have

made an excellent rock-garden plant. Another typically Mediterranean species found here and there in this range, though rather
more characteristic of the foothills of the Sierras, is the shrubby
globularia (*Globularia alypum*) growing quite dwarf here, with
neat lilac powder-puff flowers.

In shady areas can be found the chamois cress (*Hutchinsia
petraea*), which is widespread throughout Europe, often not far
from the rock cress *Arabis verna*, an essentially Mediterranean
member of the *Cruciferae* though closely allied to the alpine
blue rock cress (*A. caerulea*). Finally, in even more restricted
exposures among shady, damp rock fissures one or two clumps
of the endemic white primrose *Primula acaulis alba* can still be
found, and rocks not far from the Ermita de Betlen itself, in
rather more open situations, support the endemic spurge *Euphorbia maresii*. Coastal cliffs again hold a few plants of *Senecio rodriguezii*, more particularly on eastern exposures.

At the base of the limestone cliffs, pockets of rich, damp soil
hold the foxglove *Digitalis dubia*, while the northern slopes
below the cliffs, though dry and stony, are fairly thickly clothed
in palmeto/*Ampelodesmus* scrub, among which can be found
many interesting plants. These are mainly of the *Papilionaceae*,
and include local forms of the lovely carmine-flowered pea
Lathyrus clymenum, the clover-like *Dorycnium hirsutum*, various
bird's-foot trefoils including the endemic *Lotus tetraphyllus* and
the restharrows *Ononis reclinata* and *O. minutissima*, often to be
found growing together in rain-worn holes in the bare limestone rock—a background which sets off their yellow and pink
flowers to perfection. Among these eye-catching beauties,
another small endemic vetch is likely to pass unnoticed: this is
the slender-leaved *Hippocrepis balearica*, with minute yellowish-
white flowers, perhaps the most undistinguished of all the indigenous plants.

Below these slopes on the north face of the peninsula, arid
stony waste ground holds a great variety of annual spurges,
clovers and vetches, well worth investigating, while at the base
of the peninsula maquis vegetation holds the broom *Genista*

lucida, the flaxes *Linum gallicum* and *L. strictum*, and a variety of orchids including *Aceras*, together with very floriferous plants of *Erica multiflora*. All this area is a 'must' for the keen botanist.

THE FLORA OF THE SIERRAS

Typically, the flowers of the north-western mountain chain come into bloom about a month to six weeks later than the corresponding lowland plants, so that probably the best time to visit this area is late May or early June, by which time the flora of the plains is well past its best. However, as it is here that nearly thirty of the endemic species find refuge, the serious botanist will obviously find the later visit most rewarding.

Of the mountain flowers, Puig Major, being the tallest peak, boasts the greatest variety, but Puig de L'Ofre, Masanella close by Gorg Blau, and Ternellas further north-east are all worth a visit. During the last decade, access to much of the heights of Puig Major has been restricted, due to the presence of the long-range radar station on its summit, so that it cannot be said with any certainty what remains of its once unique flora. Knoche recorded the two endemics *Primula acaulis alba* and *Rannuculus weyleri* growing in deep shade within a few metres of the summit in the 1920s, and the former still survives, but the fate of the buttercup is less certain: this latter was of particular interest, since Knoche found its closest relatives to be among the *Ranunculaceae* of Australasia, suggesting the possibility of a land connection with that continent in former eras.

Most of the other endemics appear to be in less critical state, and are not confined to so restricted an area. In general, the sun-facing exposures of the higher peaks support an uneasy association of the two ever-present 'hedgehogs' *Astragalus poterium* and *Teucrium subspinosum*, which vie for dominance, while the congested *Smilax aspera balearica* occupies sun-baked crevices, often in association with the Mediterranean spurge, and this group hold dominion down the south-east slopes to about 3,611ft (1,100m), the altitude at which *Cistus* maquis first appears, not far above the tree-line. Again, close examination of the garigue will disclose a number of small herbaceous plants, including several of the *Leguminosae*. The spiny restharrow (*Ononis spinosa antiquorum*) becomes fairly common at slightly lower altitudes, and the very attractive and floriferous large yellow restharrow (*O. natrix*) forms bushes up to 20in (½m) high, that even grace the roadsides: some fine plants occur on the south-east side of the tunnel through Puig Major at about 2,626ft (800m). This must surely be one of the most neat and attractive of all Mediterranean plants, were it not for its horribly sticky leaves.

Two other endemics can be found on these sunny slopes: these are the large yellow-flowered umbellifer *Pastinaca lucida* with dark green leaves (well-developed plants of which may reach to 7ft (2m) when growing in deep soil), and less frequently the beautiful yellow crucifer *Brassica balearica*. Both occur not far from roadside verges, but are much more typical of the north-west-facing slopes, in semi-shade. This is in fact the situation favoured by the great majority of the mountain endemics. Near the Soller end of the Puig Major tunnel both these species occur, and not far away the rather straggly but large-flowered sandwort *Arenaria balearica* can be found, while *Cyclamen balearicum* fills the crevices with its dull grey-green marbled leaves, and damper, shady areas support masses of the small yellow-flowered *Sibthorpia balearica*, these latter two species occupying similar situations throughout most of the more northerly stretches of the Sierras.

The beds of the torrents that only flow during the rainy season provide a happy hunting ground for the botanist, since in addition to their own characteristic flora they often contain plants that have been washed down from greater altitudes. In these shady gorges, for example, *Pastinaca lucida* and *Astragalus poterium* descend almost to sea level (the latter being particularly prominent in the Ternellas Valley). Typical of the stony debris of the torrent beds (though of increasingly rare occurrence in recent years) are the paeony *Paeonia cambessedesii*, the two hellebores *Helleborus lividus* and *H. foetidus*, and the small, pale-flowered foxglove *Digitalis dubia*, that rarely exceeds 1½ft (½m) in height. Here also occur a number of mulleins, including the uncommon endemic *Verbascum boerhavii*, and clumps of the neat, pink-flowered storksbill *Erodium chamaedryoides* that is rarely without a few flowers even in the middle of winter, while a number of toadflaxes and delphiniums with, more occasionally, *Saxifraga tridactylites* form associations suggesting strong affinities with the Tyrrhenian Islands, and the possibility of an easterly land bridge in bygone times. Occasionally the endemic *Phlomis balearicus*, and the now quite rare narrow-leaved germander *Teucrium lancifolium* descend from the summits to these more modest elevations on shady screes in gorges, while the very humid atmosphere of the Gorg Blau, which retains water virtually throughout the year, provides one of the few remaining sites of the second endemic St John's wort, *Hypericum cambessedesii*, a close relative of the stinking tutsan (*H. hircinium*), which is quite widespread around the Mediterranean. In addition, shady ravines nearby hold the rather delicate violet *Viola odorata jaubertiana*, which could well be overlooked as it tends to flower rather early in the spring, and other larger flowered variants of *V. odorata*, some of which are in bloom before February is out.

The main constituents of the undergrowth of the shady areas of woodland have already been mentioned, with the exception of the autumn-flowering shrubby violet *V. arborescens*, but rock crevices under thin but shady woodland harbour *Arum muscivorum*, and various *Geranium* and *Erodium* species including masses of herb robert (*Geranium robertianum*), which must be one of the most widespread plants on the island. Several sedums, notably *S. dasyphyllum* also occur, together with a variety of *Compositae* and some bulbous plants referred to later.

Relatively deep, damp soil at the foot of the north-facing scarps is the true home of the foxglove and hellebores, together with *Pastinaca lucida* and the rare *Scutellaria balearica*, an attractive little plant with its rather large skullcap flowers usually of a bluish-purple colour, albeit rather variable. This latter plant can be found not far from the Gorg Blau, but is usually quite thinly scattered. The scarps themselves hold much of interest, including the sandworts *Arenaria balearica* and *A. grandiflora*, *Phlomis balearica*, the nearly white-flowered scabious *Scabiosa cretica* and the closely related *Cephalaria balearica*, together with the catchfly *Silene mollissima* and various rock-loving bedstraws, while the restharrows *Ononis reclinata* and *O. minutissima* are again well represented.

At greater altitudes, approaching the peaks, a more typically sub-alpine flora begins to make its appearance, including the shrubby white cinquefoil (*Potentilla caulescens*) and a variety of small cresses with *Arabis verna*, *A. hirsuta*, *Clypeola jonthlaspi*, *Thlaspi perfoliatum*, *T. arvensis* and *Draba verna*—not that these species themselves are in any sense confined to high land, being of fairly general distribution on waste land, but rather indicating that the terrain is becoming less favourable for other plants. The impression is reinforced by the blue moor grass (*Sesleria coerula*), and in the more northerly areas stands of the viviparous form of the meadow grass (*Poa bulbosa*), in which the terminal part of the flower spike consists of miniature complete plants, which can be shed and scattered ready to grow on as soon as they fall. Another plant more typical of higher altitudes in the north, is the small pink-flowered *Erinus alpinus*, which favours semi-shade in the region of some of the peaks.

Endemics in this higher region of north-facing scarps, in addition to those already mentioned, include the main concentrations of the large yellow-flowered *Brassica balearica* and the pale-flowered kidney vetch *Anthyllis balearica*, while the tough waxy leaves of the umbellifers *Pimpinella tragium balearica* and *Bupleurum barceloi* are frequent on some peaks, and the calamint *Calamentha rouyana* is still to be found in at least one area, though local form of the grey-branched broom *Genista acanthoclados* that used to occur in some of the particularly arid areas is probably now extinct. Another, more cut-leaved umbellifer, *Ligusticum huteri*, occurs here and there, and quite substantial colonies of the yellow-flowered *Crepis triasii* can be

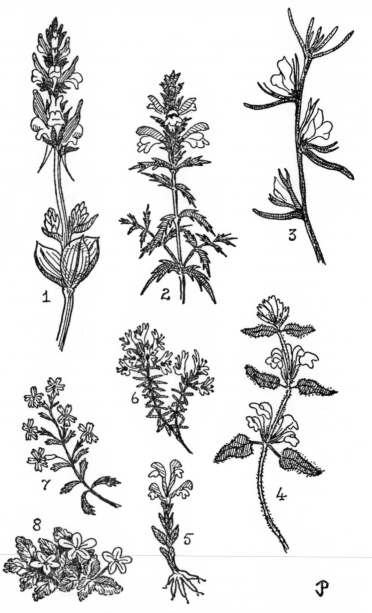

Figure 7 1 *Linaria triphylla*; 2 *Bellardia trixago*; 3 *Antirrhinum orontium*;
4 *Phlomis italica*; 5 *Scutellaria balearica*; 6 *Coris monspeliensis*; 7 *Erinus alpinus*; 8 *Erodium chamaedryoides*

found flourishing among the peaks, together with the hawk-weed *Hieracium lawsonii*, which is much rarer in the Balearics, though occurring elsewhere in Europe.

Lastly, among the rocks at moderate elevations occur a variety of bulbous- and tuberous-rooted denizens of the garigue, including the rather delicate *Narcissus tazetta* and a variety of orchids, with *Aceras* spp, *Cephalanthera longifolia*, the pyramid orchid *Anacamptis pyramidalis*, the huge *Himantoglossum longibracteatum* which can reach at least to 20in ($\frac{1}{2}$m) in height, and *Orchis italica*, *O. intacta*, *O. mascula* and *O. tridentata*. It is also impossible to overlook the beautiful slender white bells of *Allium subhirsutum* that frequent the shady rock faces and gorges, seeming rather reluctant to venture out into the dry garigue with which the onions are more usually associated.

THE FLORA OF THE COASTAL SAND DUNES

Plant communities of the littoral zone surrounding the Mediterranean basin contain many species found in similar localities in the British Isles, but the British botanist visiting the Balearics will find in addition to many old favourites, a number of new and interesting plants to delight him. Of this zone, the dune flora will usually be found to be the most prolific, and while the specialist can sort out the intricacies of the more sober-hued spurges and plantains, the casual tourist can hardly fail to be fascinated by the multi-coloured carpet of trefoils, buglosses, dwarf valerians and others that cover the ground in sheltered hollows—the Mediterranean counterparts of bird's-foot trefoil (*Lotus corniculatus*)/bloody cranesbill (*Geranium sanguineum*) association. Also worthy of more than a passing glance are a number of attractive plants notable for their colour and form of foliage, including some familiar rock-garden favourites.

Fine dune formations stabilised by a well-developed covering of vegetation are to be found in the Bays of Pollensa and Alcudia in the north-east, and some more restricted areas in the south-west and south-east, but the extensive dunes that used to line the Bay of Palma have largely been replaced by flourishing and ever-expanding holiday resorts, while but little remains of the once extensive area of saltmarsh, the Prat, that once lay behind them. Most stretches of dunes support a basic type of flora that does, however, differ appreciably in detail from area to area due in part to minor local climatic variations. In the vicinity of C'an Picafort and the Albufera, the soil is of a rather more siliceous, moisture-retentive composition than in other areas, supporting perhaps the greatest variety of plants, but the beach in the Bay of Pollensa is also worthy of inspection, as here can be found growing plants typical of the mountain garigue, looking distressingly out of character, having been transported down from the heights by the Torrente de San Jordi that empties into the bay. Perhaps the most interesting south coast dunes occur in the vicinity of Campos, particularly notable for the various sun roses (*Helianthemum* spp) that they support, some of quite restricted distribution.

The seaward-facing flanks of many dunes have a thin covering of marram grass (*Ammophila arenaria*) and also support the purple spurge (*Euphorbia peplis*) and the sea spurge (*E. paralias*), the latter with thick fleshy leaves that tend to lie close round the stem to cut down moisture loss, and give the plant a strikingly columnar appearance in the earlier stages of growth. The endemic *E. pithyusa*, though more typical of the inland garigue, occurs rather sparingly on most of the dunes. Other xerophytic plants that are of rather more cosmopolitan distribution in the coastal regions include the grey-green spiny sea holly (*Eryngium maritimum*) which is quite common in a number of areas, though patchily distributed in others, together with the well-known sea rocket (*Cakile maritima*) and the rather more localised sea stock (*Matthiola sinuata*). The very similar but rather larger-petalled three-horned stock (*M. tricuspidata*) a more typically Mediterranean species is much more widespread: unfortunately, unlike its garden relative, it is completely odourless.

Less attractive, but none the less interesting from a botanical point of view, are the various plantains to be found on the dunes, notably the stag's horn and sea plantains (*Plantago coronopus* and *P. maritima*). Though of no floral value, plants of the former species can often reach up to 20in ($\frac{1}{2}$m) in diameter, and are well worth a second glance on account of the beautiful symmetry of form that they can display. The deeply cut leaves and the flower stems grow radially outwards, flat on the sand, and the flower spikes then turn erect to give a bowl-like outline.

More confined to the landward-facing slopes of the dunes sheltered from the salt spray are a variety of brilliantly coloured ground-hugging plants. Prominent among these are masses of the southern bird's-foot trefoil (*Lotus creticus*), the bright yellow, flame-shot flowers of which contrast vividly with the various blues and purples of the buglosses *Echium arenarium* and *E. creticum*, and less frequent patches of the pale pink dwarf valerian *Valerianella echinata*, while the yellow hawk's-beard *Crepis bulbosa* is scattered everywhere. Though the grey-leaved southern bird's-foot trefoil is easily the most abundant and widespread of the *Leguminosae* to be found on the dunes, large patches of the more lush *Medicago littoralis*, with sulphur-yellow flowers in clustered heads set against green leaflets, are quite plentiful in some areas, but the trailing woolly grey-foliaged sea medick (*M. marina*) so typical of Mediterranean shores seems distinctly less plentiful than it was in former years, apparently having given way to the trefoil.

Scattered over this floral carpet are numerous mounds of two familiar rock-garden plants both prized for their attractive foliage: these are the yellow 'everlasting' *Helichrysum stoechas* and the germander *Teucrium polium*. The former makes a brilliant display during late spring with pure deep yellow buttons clustered tightly above stems and foliage of shining silver, but the germander is much more variable and less reliable. Though all forms have felted silver-grey foliage, the small flowers vary from an insignificant off-white to a rather pale purple. There is, however, a much more attractive endemic form with more slender leaves, compact growth, and

Figure 8   1 *Echium arenarium*; 2 *Medicago marina*; 3 *Lotus creticus*; 4 *Helichrysum stoechas*; 5 *Asteriscus maritimus*; 6 *Thymelaea hirsuta*; 7 *Thymelaea tartonraira*

rather larger flowerheads usually of a reddish-purple colour. It is less common in the littoral zone (though there are a few areas that it favours, often among pines), preferring the hilly areas of the north-east, where it flowers as early as March, and will usually be past its best by the time the tourist season is at its height. Providing it is hardy, this variety should prove to be a much better bet for the rock-garden enthusiast!

Some select areas, notably along the east and south coasts still support colonies of the beautiful white sea daffodil (*Pancratium maritimum*), which, unfortunately, is likely to be missed by most flower-hunters, as it has a very late flowering season. Other bulbous species are few, though the tassel hyacinth (*Muscari comosum*) at times infiltrates on to the coastal dunes, together with various wild garlics, principally the rose garlic (*Allium roseum*), but also including a small pale form of garlic that looks like a possible hybrid between the previous species and the pure white *A. subhirsutum*. This plant is well developed in the region of Pto de Pollensa.

A number of dunes, notably those of the north-east, support an interesting shrub association. Dominant are the junipers, *Juniperus oxycedrus* around the Bay of Alcudia, but principally *J. phoenicea* elsewhere, followed by two interesting close relatives of the daphnes, *Thymelaea hirsuta* and *T. tartonraira* respectively. The latter has a typical shrubby habit, with grey, felted leaves and small insignificant yellow flowers, but the taller *T. hirsuta* has small thick fleshy green leaves pressed around the stem in typical xerophytic fashion, and the clusters of yellow flowers at the tips of the branches appear rather more prominent as a consequence. If one tries to pull off a stem to press, the usual result is that the bark and leaves strip off, leaving the tough stem fibres intact: in former times, these used to be employed in rope manufacture. This is altogether a curious plant, for when young, the whole plant has a lax, trailing appearance, and in fact when growing among the dunes it could be mistaken at first glance for sea purslane (*Honkenya peploides*). Among these shrubs appear the sun roses (*Helianthemum* spp) and the ever-present asphodel, and the whole intergrades gradually with cistus maquis as one proceeds further inland.

Damp depressions are not infrequent among the dunes, some being of a markedly saline character, but others holding water above a hard pan of mainly calcareous salts. These latter areas are often characterised by the presence of tamarisk (*Tamarix gallica*) which almost forms small woods in some favoured sites, and not infrequently by myrtle. A variety of rushes also occurs, including the sea rush (*Juncus maritimus*), sharp sea rush (*J. acutus*) and the black bog rush (*Schoenus nigricans*)—the latter being a species particularly fond of calcareous soils. The round-headed club-rush (*Scirpus haloschoenus*) is quite plentiful in most of these areas, but the sea club-rush (*S. maritimus*) is rather more frequent along the south coast. Another bulbous species also appears in these humid troughs, this being the triquetrous garlic (*Allium triquetrum*) with a rather stout, triangular stem, and large drooping white bells. More saline areas support sea lavenders (*Statice* spp)—mainly *S. virgata* on clayey soil, and *S. legrandii* in the vicinity of the Albufera, together with a wider variety of plantains including the typical Mediterranean *Plantago lagopus* and *P. crassifolia*, though the multi-headed *P. psyllium* prefers the mouths of the few permanent watercourses, where it can find rather less saline conditions which are more to its liking.

Many of the better developed stretches of dunes are backed by extensive pinewoods, and an account of the variety of orchids found therein has already been given, but clearings behind the dunes particularly in rather damp depressions support an interesting association of the centaury (*Centaurium pulchellum*) and its close relative, the yellow-wort (*Blackstonia perfoliata*), while around the Bay of Alcudia, the much less frequent yellow centaury (*C. maritimum*) also occurs. The bright pinks and yellows of these members of the gentian family often occur alongside patches of the red and blue pimpernels (*Anagallis* spp), where they combine to paint an unforgettable canvas on the sandy soil. Here also can be found that familiar small white

Page 71 (above) The endemic St John's wort, *Hypericum balearicum*; (below) *Helleborus foetidus* growing by the roadside

Page 72 (*left*) The tall grass *Ampelodesmus mauritanicus*; (*below*) the most characteristic plant of Majorca, the asphodel *Asphodelus micro-carpus*

crucifer, sweet alison (*Lobularia maritima*), so often used in our gardens as a border plant, and some of the annual flax species, while in some areas can be found the very local autumn-flowering shrubby violet (*Viola arborescens*).

SEA CLIFFS AND COASTAL ROCKS

Though generally poor in vegetative cover, the rockier stretches of coastline shelter a variety of interesting plants, particularly on their more accessible exposures. Wherever any patches of sandy soil have been able to collect in crevices, sea lavenders will be found—mainly *Statice virgata*, though in the north-east and on the seaward-facing slopes of the Sierras *S. duruscula* is rather more typical. Less frequent, though almost confined to this type of habitat are the endemics *Paeonia cambessedesii*, *Helichrysum lamarckii* and *Senecio rodriguesii*, already noted as occurring on the Formentor Peninsula. They generally require rather deeper crevices, however, and do not often descend much below 330ft (100m) or so. It might be added at this point that considerable stretches of sea cliff along the north-east coast are very inaccessible, and still largely unexplored, so that there is no knowing what the adventurous wanderer may still find in these remote, wilder areas.

The rocky shore near the base of the Arta Peninsula supports a rather greater variety of plants. Here *Asteriscus martimus* holds its small marigolds neatly set over tight mounds of foliage growing on almost bare rock, and looks a most attractive and desirable plant: on richer soil, however, it becomes an untidy, straggling weed. Here also species of the mountain garigue reach right down to sea level; *Sonchus spinosus* grows on rock platforms almost washed by salt spray, and *Cyclamen balearicum* can be found massed in shady crevices and gullies.

SALTMARSHES

The areas of the Salinas at Colonia de San Jordi and the Al-
E

bufera support plant communities quite typical of the common Mediterranean saltmarsh associations, in which the golden samphire (*Inula crithmoides*), the glasswort (*Salicornia fruticosa*) and sea-blite (*Suaeda maritima*) are prominent, with the various sea lavenders being well represented. The sea aster (*Aster tripolium*) and triquetrous garlic (*Allium triquetrum*) frequent the marshy verges in the more saline areas, while plantains in variety and the occasional tamarisk (*Tamarix gallica*) indicate the presence of fresher water, thus giving a useful guide to the variations in salinity throughout the marshes, which also affects the distribution of molluscs and aquatic insects. Rushes of the marshes include the pale yellow-green sea rush (*Juncus maritimus*), the bright-brown sharp sea rush (*J. acutus*) and the small, starry toad rush (*J. bufonius*), all of which will be familiar to British botanists, together with the round-headed club-rush (*Scirpus holoschoenus*). The sedges, a group notoriously difficult to identify, have little of interest to offer in the lowland areas of either salt- or fresh-water, though the specialist may find greater variety including one or two unusual species in the damper areas of the Sierras, notably in the vicinity of the Gorg Blau.

FLOWERS OF THE WAYSIDE AND WASTELAND

It is here that the casual tourist is likely to realise the true wealth of the Mediterranean flora, and be impressed by its beauty. Walking along country roads during April or May, or even on coach trips around the island, he cannot fail to remark on the variety of wild flowers that he will see by the roadside. Those who delay their visit until June may well be disappointed by the withered roadside vegetation scorched by the mid-day sun, but a trip into the mountains will soon disclose many of the lowland plants still in flower, though not in such great profusion. Following the heat of summer, many plants have a second flowering with the advent of the autumnal rainy season that usually starts late in September, and indeed a few select species only flower in this damp spell towards the close of the year. But these few apart, the lover of wild flowers should visit Majorca during the spring months, when the island is at its best. True, February may hold its own particular appeal, when all the lowlands are covered in delicate almond blossom that falls like snow before the gusty winds of March, and in this latter month the ever-blooming rosemary may combine with a few precocious spring flowers to add variety to the varied shades of green. But it is not until the real heat of the Mediterranean sun begins to make itself felt early in April that the fields suddenly erupt into a multi-coloured carpet of flowers.

On the richer soils of the central plain, and particularly in the south-east, the roadsides are alive with the pale yellow sorrel flowers of that most beautiful and yet most persistent of all weeds, the rashly introduced Bermuda buttercup (*Oxalis pes-caprae*), while the deeper orange-yellow of the field marigold (*Calendula arvensis*) mingle with the intermediate shades of the larger crown daisy (*Chrysanthemum coronatum*) and its paler, bi-coloured variety *C. c. discolor* which occur in much more compact clumps. This range of varying shades of yellow is startlingly offset by the frequent clumps of borage (*Borago officinalis*), the even more vivid and deeper blues of the alkanets (*Anchusa italica* and *A. officinalis*), and the bright carpets of red poppies (*Papaver rhoeas*, *P. dubium* and *P. hybridum*). Other large plants that cannot fail to catch the eye include the ever-present pearly white spires of the asphodel (*Asphodelus microcarpus*), the tall tree mallow (*Lavatera arborea*) that can attain well over 7ft (2m) in stature, together with other smaller species, and the large, spreading crinkly leaved mullein *Verbascum sinuatum*, together with its smaller close relative, the more densely spiked dark mullein (*V. nigrum*). In drier areas, plants of the low maquis, principally rosemary and the various rock roses make a significant and colourful contribution to the roadside flora.

Many stretches of wasteland and stony verge are covered knee-deep in luxuriant stands of mustards (*Sinapis* spp) and the wild radish (*Raphanus raphanistrum*) in a variety of delicate pastel shades of yellow, cream and shell-pink that make a most welcome addition to the general picture, and serve to highlight the more brilliant colours. Turning from beauty of colour to beauty of form, the delightful variegated foliage of the slender, thistle-like *Galactites tomentosa*, with fluffy flowerheads ranging from almost cerise through pale pink to pure white must surely take pride of place, while the heavy armoury of the milk thistle (*Silybum marianum*) that can reach to nearly 7ft (2m), and the similar but smaller and more compact cardoon (*Cynara cardunculus*) with characteristic globular flowerheads surrounded by leathery, spiny grey-green bracts uncomfortably large for the size of the plant are unlikely to go unnoticed.

Before taking a closer look at the smaller flowering plants of the waste places, it is worth mentioning two foreign introductions that will certainly attract the attention of visitors to the island. The first and more important of these is the so-called prickly pear (*Opuntia ficus-indica*), a true cactus brought into Europe, it is believed, by Christopher Columbus. It is cultivated quite extensively in the Balearics, where it forms both a hedging plant and a valuable foodstuff, since the ripe fruits are edible. The other, the agave or century plant (*Agave americana*) was introduced not long afterwards, principally for ornamental value, as a hedging plant, but has since naturalised, and is now widespread in a variety of habitats. The enormous arching, leathery grey-green leaves can reach 7ft (2m) and once in its lifetime, usually after about ten years, a flower spike shoots up very rapidly to a height of 33ft (10m) or more. After flowering, the whole plant usually dies, though offshoots may arise from the basal rosette. It is interesting to note in passing that the habit and life-cycle of this plant is closely akin to those of some of the dwarf alpine saxifrages so prized for the rock garden, yet the two are completely unrelated.

Turning to the host of smaller plants that invite closer inspection at almost every suitable stopping point along the roadsides, it is impossible to single out and do justice to more than a few. Mention has already been made of the carpets of trefoils, buglosses, pimpernels and the like that cover open sandy areas with a riot of colour during the spring months. As the soil improves in richness, and becomes more water-retentive, an increasing variety of species make their appearance. Perhaps this flora is seen at its best in the region between Arta and Pollensa, though the basin around Soller has much to recommend it, and possibly can boast a greater variety of the more moisture-loving species, and the rarer herbaceous lowland plants.

Beginning with the bulbous plants, *Allium roseum*, the rose garlic bears repetition, as does the delicate white, but more local *A. subhirsutum*, though the tall purple mop-heads of *A. rotundum* are likely to meet the eye first, accompanied by the pale-flowered *A. paniculatum*. The blue tassel hyacinth (*Muscari comosum*) is scattered quite liberally on waste ground throughout the islands, but both the familiar white star-of-Bethlehem (*Ornithogallum umbellatum*) one of the most beautiful of all bulbous plants, and the deep carmine spikes of the field gladiolus (*Gladiolus segetum*) are more frequently found in areas of richer soil. The very similar *G. illyricus* occurs in a greater variety of sites, being perhaps more typical of the mountain slopes, notably in the vicinity of Soller. It is distinguished by having rather fewer, more widely spaced flowers arranged all around the stem, instead of in a one-sided arched raceme.

Perhaps one of the most attractive of the smaller plants to occur commonly by the roadsides is the glaucous-leaved three-leaved toadflax (*Linaria triphylla*). A variable species this, in which the best colour forms have flowers patterned in white, yellow and royal purple. It makes an excellent subject for colour photography, as do the cream and purple pyramids of *Bellardia trixago*, a close relative of the bartsias. A further member of the *Scrophulariaceae* widely distributed on waste ground is *Antirrhinum orontium*, a slender, pink-flowered snapdragon that is also quite attractive in its own more subdued fashion—much more so than is implied in its unfortunate common name of weasel's snout.

A number of the parasitic broomrapes occur not infrequently by the wayside, most of which are parasitic on members of the

pea family. Prominent amongst these is the branched broom-
rape (*Orobanche ramosa*), the rather lax, blue flower spikes of
which can be found also on plantains and the lentisk in particular from early spring up to late June. Later in the summer,
the rather similar endemic O. *balearica* can be found by careful
searching, principally in more shady areas, and often on ivy
(*Hedera helix*).

The *Leguminosae*, host plants for the broomrapes, are particularly well distributed in the Balearics, including *Ononis* (7
spp), *Medicago* (16 spp), *Trifolium* (20 spp), *Lotus* (10 spp), *Vicia*
(c 15 spp) and *Lathyrus* (c 10 spp) among others, together with
numerous local varieties and polymorphic species. Many of these
require expert identification, but a number are quite easy and
likely to attract the attention. Of these, the bright crimson
solitary flowers of the red vetchling (*Lathyrus cicera*) can be
singled out for special mention: they are widespread among the
more lush stands of vegetation from early March onwards. The
deep-carmine everlasting pea (*L. latifolius*) is a lover of humidity,
and its beautiful large flowers must be sought along the banks
of irrigation ditches and similar damp sites, though occasionally
also found straggling through hedgerows and thickets. Though
slightly smaller, *L. clymenum* is possibly even more attractive than
the latter, with a bright carmine standard and pale bluish-mauve
keel, that in the best forms can be almost pure white. Both this
and the rather larger-flowered form *L. c. articulatus* are very
variable in form and colour, and are somewhat more typical of
drier sandy hillsides, as is another southern species, the narrow-
leaved red vetchling (*L. setifolius*), with smaller, brick-red flowers.

Most of the *Vicia* and *Lotus* species are to be found either in the
mountains or in the littoral zone, but of the medicks, *Medicago
rigidula* and *M. orbicularis* are circum-Mediterranean species of
quite general distribution in lowland areas of the Balearics. In
addition, the islands support a variety of interesting clovers, of
which the star clover (*Trifolium stellatum*) is perhaps the most
widespread and the most easily recognised. After the flowers fall
the sepals spread wide and assume a dark red colour with a

white 'eye', that is quite characteristic and cannot be over-looked. Many other species are of quite localised Mediterranean distribution. Both the horseshoe vetches *Hippocrepis unisiliquosa* and *H. multisiliquosa* occur (though the latter is much less common), as does *Scorpiurus muricatus*, a common weed with small yellow flowers and most un-vetchlike entire leaves. All these legumes are well worth examining after flowering is over, to see the strange contortions that develop in the seed pods on ripening, prior to ejection of the seeds. Finally in this family, passing mention must be made of the blue-flowered pitch trefoil (*Psoralea bituminosa*) that straggles for yards through thick herbage and hedgerows by the roadsides. The leaves when bruised give off a strong tarry odour.

The mignonette (*Reseda alba*) is quite a feature of the more floriferous verges, where its whitish spires comfortably out-number its smaller relative, the pale yellow *R. lutea*. The bright blue flowers of chicory (*Cichorium intybus*) are quite regular, and other shades of blue are provided by the scabious *Scabiosa maritima* of widespread lowland distribution, particularly near the coast. A variable plant this, the flowers of which can range through pale mauve to pink, though the more local *S. stellata* is usually a more definite blue. Wild clary (*Salvia verbenacea*) pro-vides deeper shades, though this is another polymorphic species.

Other members of the mint family are well represented, par-ticularly in damper areas, where considerable variation is found among individuals of this notorious group. Germanders (*Teuc-rium* spp) are more typical of the mountains and the littoral, but there are a few interesting lowland varieties. The specialist, however, is more likely to be interested in the small thyme-like sub-shrubs of the genus *Micromeria* which contains a number of species of localised Mediterranean distribution, together with the endemic *M. rodriguesii* which is quite plentiful in some drier, stony areas.

Catchflys are quite common, with the large-flowered *Silene cucubalus* well represented, and the small, red-flowered *S. gallica* very plentiful. This latter is another very variable plant, shading through to pure white on occasions. Mention must also be made of the delicate love-in-a-mist (*Nigella damascena*) the bright blue flowers of which seem to be becoming increasingly scarce. Walls everywhere are covered in spring with masses of virgin's bower (*Clematis cirrhosa*), which at this season is covered with fluffy white seedheads.

A brief word or two now on a number of less conspicuous Mediterranean species that could easily be overlooked, yet are of some interest. The nettle-leaved figwort (*Scrophularia peregrina*) with its small deep red-brown flowers could easily be mistaken for one of the British species, while the multi-headed branched plantain (*Plantago psyllium*) though of fairly widespread European distribution, may be unfamiliar to British visitors, and is easily overlooked. A series of small grey-leaved sub-shrubs of the genus *Phagnalon*, though of little floral interest, have attractive foliage, and could be mistaken for the much more desirable *Helichrysums* when out of flower.

Turning to the *Compositae*, a roadside plant likely to attract the attention is *Urospermum dalechampii*, which stands out among the hawkweeds by reason of its large, pale lemon-yellow, many-petalled flowerheads. These often have a dark centre, but must not be mistaken for members of the genus *Tolpis*: their identification is easily settled by reference to the swelling of the stem just below the flowerhead. An interesting thistle very typical of the Mediterranean region is *Xanthium spinosum*, with attractive greyish foliage and starry radiating straw-coloured spines, not exactly a floral beauty, but of interesting design. Thinking of texture in plants immediately brings to mind the hare's-foot plantain (*Plantago lagopus*) with silky blue-grey oval flowerheads poised gracefully erect over slender spreading leaves. This in turn brings recollections of the hare's-tail grass (*Lagurus ovatus*), with similar-shaped heads of an attractive pale straw yellow and an almost woolly texture, that occurs on sandy soil notably in the bays of the north-east. Another equally striking, though rather more plentiful grass of the fields, is the unmistakable *Aegilops ovata*, with characteristically bulbous flower spikelets.

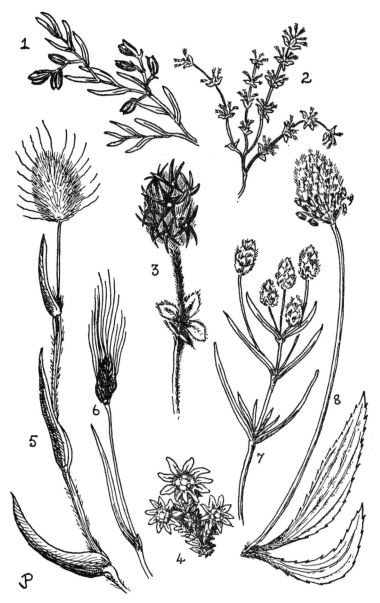

Figure 9 1 *Polygala rupestris*; 2 *Micromeria rodriguesii*; 3 *Trifolium stellatum*; 4 *Evax pygmaea*; 5 *Lagarus ovatus*; 6 *Aegilops ovata*; 7 *Plantago indica*; 8 *Plantago lagopus*

Finally, to what I regard as the most magnificent of all the Majorcan wild flowers, the mallow-flowered bindweed (*Convolvulus althaeoides*). If on the island April is the month of the asphodel and the rock rose, then May certainly belongs to the convolvulus, and of this genus pride of place must surely go to the superb deep pink trumpets of *C. althaeoides*. No superlatives can lavish too high praise on this magnificent plant that is equally happy trailing alongside country roads or climbing up through shrubs of the lower maquis, that become wreathed in glowing pink throughout the last days of spring.

CHAPTER FOUR

Non-flowering plants

HERE WE ENTER a field of study that for many years has been regarded as essentially the province of the specialist botanist. This view has been based on the considerable difficulty of identification that many of the species present. Indeed this difficulty is not to be minimised, for many of the mosses and smaller fungi require microscopic examination in order to confirm their identity. Further, attempts at 'popularising' identification often have to be based on features of form, structure and texture that are difficult to describe.

In recent years, however, improvements in colour printing techniques have resulted in the publication of a number of attractively (and more important, accurately) illustrated colour guides to the fungi, ferns and mosses with the result that more and more amateur naturalists are taking an interest in these fascinating groups of plants. Even if specific identification remains difficult in some cases (and this will be so for a number of Majorcan species of fungi, notably the endemics and those of a more restricted southerly distribution in Europe which have not yet found their way into the popular literature), this should not act as too great a deterrent. The amateur will still find that with a little practice he will be able to place most plants into their correct family or genus, and this alone can yield much valuable ecological information, particularly if combined with notes on habitat, seasonal appearance, etc.

The most comprehensive lists of non-flowering plants of Majorca appear to be those compiled by Knoche in the early 1930s, to which there have been few more recent additions—indeed it seems likely that the continued clearing of vegetation for agriculture and building will tend to decrease the humidity of the atmosphere, and this already seems to be having an adverse effect on some of the rarer shade-loving species which are in danger of extinction in the none too distant future. Against this, however, it must be emphasised that most of the collecting so far has been concentrated in the vicinity of Soller and Valldemosa, together with some of the coastal pinewoods, and there are still some humid, shady areas in the north-west Sierras that could well repay a more thorough investigation.

FUNGI

This group provides perhaps the most interesting, and certainly the most colourful subjects of this chapter, but also, unfortunately, the most difficult to locate and identify. Lacking the pigment chlorophyll, which green plants use as an aid to synthesising their own food, the fungi live a parasitic or saprophytic existence, feeding on the living or dead tissue of various host plants, which may suffer considerable damage and often eventual death in the process. The *mycelium*, a cobwebby structure that contains the food-absorbing organs, may remain hidden in the ground or in the tissues of the host plant for many months until favourable conditions occur for the formation of the characteristic fruiting bodies by which the fungi are usually identified. Most species appear above ground during the rainy season in autumn, though a few prefer the rather shorter damp season in spring. Should either prove too dry, however, it is not uncommon for the plant to delay fruiting for a whole year or more. Consequently, the list of some 290 different varieties of fungi produced by Knoche could well represent only a fraction of the total there to be discovered, and there is doubtless much scope for the amateur to lend valuable assistance in this field. As an aid to identification, a colour photograph of any unusual species should be taken, together with notes on colour (which may be very misleading in a photograph, particularly if the exposure has not been absolutely accurate), gill form if appropriate, spore pattern (see textbooks), colour and texture of flesh, effect of bruising, and smell. Taste is also useful, but is not to be recommended for the inexperienced amateur, or in the case of unfamiliar species, since some fungi can be quite deadly even in fairly small quantities.

Two species of considerable importance to the islanders because of their attacks on citrus trees are the familiar yellowish-brown honey fungus (*Armillaria mellea*), parasitic on the roots of orange trees in particular and often causing their eventual death, and a small species *Rosellinia wolffensteniani* that does a lot of damage to the actual fruit crop. A number of encrusting fungi of the genera *Corticium* and *Sterium* attack the stem and branches, together with a few of the much larger polypores, of which the greyish, bracket-shaped *Phallinus igniarius*, and the shaggy, russet-brown *Inonotus hispidus* are typical. The grey-brown, leathery *Daedalia biennis*, of rather more restricted distribution, occurs on decaying orchard trees, but may not attack living tissue. A smaller, bracket-shaped gill fungus *Schizophyllum alneum* is also very common in orchards and indeed in all types of drier woodland in winter and early spring.

Of the *Ascomycetes*, an order that contains the cup fungi, club fungi and various encrusting species, many of which grow on decaying timber, the genera *Peziza*, *Strickeria* and *Pleospora* are well represented, the two latter groups in particular containing a number of species believed to be endemic to the Balearics. They are best noted and identified by reference to the host plants on which they occur, and include *Strickeria marina* on the sea squill (*Urginea maritima*) and *Strickeria marina euphorbiae* on the dead stems of some of the larger spurges. *Pleospora spinosa* attacks the branches of the spiny broom (*Calycotome infesta*) and *Pleospora gigaspora* can be found abundantly on the leaves of the asphodel (*Asphodelus microcarpus*) while *Pleospora mallorquina* is another species to favour the sea squill. Doubtless many more of these vegetative scavengers remain to be discovered in the Balearics.

The order *Basidiomycetes*, though less numerous than the *Asco-*

mycetes, contains the larger species that are more likely to attract the attention of the amateur naturalist. Before turning to this rather spectacular group, however, brief mention must be made of a genus of generally small fungi in this order which are mostly parasitic on foliage, and contain a number of endemic species: these members of the genus *Puccinia* occur on plants of the daisy family in particular, including *Sonchus spinosus*, *Hyoseris radiata*, *H. scabrae* and *Crepis* spp, and have been as yet little investigated —a job that must probably be left to the specialist, as they are difficult to separate.

With the exception of the polypores already mentioned, the majority of *Basidiomycetes* are found growing in the ground, or among rotting vegetable or animal matter. The best collecting sites are the shady north-facing wooded slopes of the Sierras, the steep rift of the Gorg Blau, and the pinewoods backing the coastal sand dunes that are often kept moist by salt-water seepage. Of the larger, more noticeable species, the tooth-fungi (*Hydnaceae*) are widely distributed in all the Balearic Islands. This group gets its name from the spine-like projections on the underside of the cap, which are a ready aid to identification, and most of the species are fairly easy to distinguish. They usually fruit in autumn, and the pale pink-buff caps of *Hydnum repandum* occur commonly in most areas of mature woodland towards the close of the year. The dark blue-black *Phellodon niger* is one of the easiest to identify; its flesh is pale blue when young, but almost black in older specimens, and it has a markedly reflexed cap that also darkens with age. The dark grey, scaly *Sarcodon imbricatum* usually has a very characteristic shaggy appearance, and is very typical of the sandy lowland stretches of pinewood, albeit rather thinly distributed in the drier areas. The familiar Chantarelle (*Cantharellus cibarius*) is abundant, but more associated with the stretches of oakwood, occurring principally at moderate elevations in the Sierras.

Members of the genus *Boletus*, characterised by the sponge-like structure of the underside of the cap formed by the open pores of the spore tubes, are also quite numerous in the mountains, and include an endemic species *B. miramar*, and others of rather local distribution in southern Europe such as *B. bellini* and *B. corsicus*. These can all be found growing on the north-west flanks of the Sierras between Valldemosa and the slopes of Puig Major. It is surprising that neither the chantarelle nor *B. luteus*, both of which are very good to eat, form any part of the Majorcan diet. This is certainly not due to any surplus of food, but more probably to a combination of fear and ignorance, as there are a number of species superficially similar to, but rather smaller than the chantarelle growing in the Balearics, some of which are rather poisonous. It is difficult to offer a similar excuse for the yellow boletus, however, as *B. luteus* is quite widespread, and usually easily distinguishable by its pale chestnut slimy cap, ochre yellow pores and purple-white stem with a prominent purple-black ring. *B. granulatus* is equally common, though perhaps more typically restricted to the pinewoods, but both cap and stalk are orange-buff, and most of the other species are distinctly darker. The majority of fungi of this genus are non-poisonous, though a few have an unpleasant bitter taste, but several make quite excellent eating, and could be used by the peasants as a dietary supplement if required.

The genera *Hygrophorus*, *Lactaria* and *Russula* are all well represented, mostly by colourful species that are of widespread European distribution, and the British naturalist will find many that are familiar to him—though often in rather unfamiliar situations. Species that in the British Isles are more typically associated with beech woods for example, grow quite happily in the Mediterranean oak forests.

Mushrooms of the genus *Agaricus* include the field mushroom (*A. campestris*) and the horse mushroom (*A. arvensis*), which appear in fields and orchards during the autumn, and are used to some extent in *tortillas* (omelettes) and more occasionally in *paella* (a rice-based dish combining chicken and seafood). This family also includes a number of other whitish mushrooms of a more essentially southerly distribution: *A. olearius* and *A. petaloides* associate with olive trees in the more mountainous areas, though the former will also be found in pinewoods. *A. opuntiae*, found on the decaying trunks of the prickly pear cactus, is of interest in that it was first described from Majorca (though it could well have been imported with the plants). Two small greyish-white members of the related genus *Volvariella* (which is renowned for throwing up many rare and local species) have been described from the vicinity of Valldemosa, *V. sollerensis* and *V. gliocephala*, of which the former is believed to be a Majorcan endemic and the other is not by any means widespread.

Inocybe and *Cortinarius* are both represented by a number of species, though only the deadly poisonous *I. fastigiata* and the rather more localised *I. destricta* in the former genus, and *Cortinarius cinnamomeus* (in a variety of colour forms) in the latter are at all common. The genus *Tricholoma* contains some interesting plants, including the bright yellow *T. sulphureum* that has a very characteristic strong tarry odour, and *T. saponaceum*, a mottled grey-brown species smelling, as its specific name suggests, of household soap: a local variety also occurs, that may warrant full specific status and is believed to be endemic.

Amanita includes the grisette (*A. vaginata*), which is another edible species, and the beautiful pure white, delicate but deadly poisonous destroying angel (*A. virosa*): both are common and widespread in autumn.

In the *Gasteromycetales*, the stinkhorn (*Phallus impudicus*) recognisable at some little distance by its nauseating smell, occurs albeit rather rarely, in woodland on the mountain flanks at moderate elevations, and this habitat also supports a number of puff-balls and earth-stars, among which the spiny puff-ball (*Lycoperdon echinatum*) and *Geastrum rufescens* are the most plentiful.

MOSSES

Knoche lists about 105 species of mosses for the Balearics, almost all of which occur in Majorca. The majority of these are fairly common and occur in characteristic associations, but as many of them require microscopic identification there is little point in

Page 89   (above left) Ophrys tenthredinifera; (above right) Ophrys bertolonii;
(below left) Narcissus tazetta; (below right) Orchis italica

Page 90 (*above*) The locust reaches Majorca fairly regularly in small numbers; (*below*) fully grown larva of the spurge hawk moth *Celerio euphorbiae*

doing more than giving the most easily recognisable members of the associations in areas where the mosses become a dominant part of the vegetative cover.

In pinewoods on sandy soil, beard mosses of the genus *Barbula* are frequent, covering much of the damper ground. *B. convoluta* and *B. muralis* are the most plentiful, the former also occurs commonly in the more saline areas, and in hollows among the dunes, where it associates with *Trichostomum flavovirens*.

Characteristic of woods with a more dense canopy are *Leucodon sciuroides*, numerous feather-mosses of the genus *Brachythecium*, varying in colour from bright green to old gold. *Hebradon perpusillus* also occurs abundantly in the oakwoods, and also flourishes along with *Fabronia pusilla* in the more open olive groves.

The most widely distributed moss of the higher altitudes in the Sierras is probably the dark green cushion moss *Grimmia orbicularis*, though it rarely ascends to the highest peaks, being more typical of the upper limit of the tree zone. The wavy feather moss (*Neckera crispa*) and hairy screw moss (*Tortula ruralis*) are two fairly common and easily identified mosses that are found at intervals right up to the summits, both being quite characteristic of limestone peaks. The beard mosses *Barbula subulatis*, *B. muraria* and *B. ruraliformis*, together with the beautiful cypress-leaved feather moss (*Hypnum cupressiforme*) also reach the 4,595ft (1,400m) mark on a number of peaks, and the feathery plumes of *Homolothecium sericeum* become widespread on limestone rocks at just below this level.

At intermediate elevations, other *Barbula* species attract attention, but are very difficult to identify. Shady valleys of high humidity below 950ft (300m) shelter a variety of species of *Bryum*, *Funaria* and *Hypnum*, including soft carpets of the golden-green plumy-crested feather moss (*Hypnum molluscum*) and *Funaria calcarea*, both species very typical of woodland that has developed on limestone formations.

F

LICHENS

Here again, the scope of this book will permit the inclusion of only a small number of selected lichens that may be taken as characteristic of the few habitats in which they are likely to attract attention. Of these, by far the most noticeable at low altitudes is the grey reindeer moss *Cladonia endivaefolia* which covers large expanses of ground in the more open sandy pine-woods. In more stony, shady areas, the closely related *C. pyxidata* is nearly as plentiful.

Rocks at the summit of the highest peaks carry a rich lichen flora, mainly composed of colourful *Verrucaria* spp, and includ-ing the dull grey *V. rupestris* and the black *V. nigrescens*, against which patches of a brilliant red endemic form of *V. marmorea* provide a startling contrast. Dominant on the higher limestone rocks, however, is the white encrusting *Aspicilia calcarea*, which exists in a variety of forms at lower levels along with a number of species that prefer shady ground, including *Cladonia pyxidata*, *Squamaria crassa*, *Xanthoria parietina* and others.

Several members of the genus *Romalina* occur on the bark of oak and pine trees in particular, and there is one endemic species, *R. knochei*, that is likely to be found on the bark of the lentisk.

FERNS

Some twenty-two species of ferns have been described for Majorca, of which three are very rare and on the verge of ex-tinction in the island. These are the prickly shield-fern (*Aspidium aculeatum*), the hard fern (*Blechnum spicant*) that can be readily picked out by its erect, herring-bone patterned fertile fronds standing up from among the spreading barren fronds, and the unmistakable hart's-tongue (*Scolopendrium vulgare*). The *Aspidium* is virtually confined to north-facing crevasses near the summit of Puig Major, where it associates with the delicate little wall rue (*Asplenium ruta-muraria*), and the common rusty-backed fern (*Ceterach officinarium*), while the common polypody (*Polypodium*

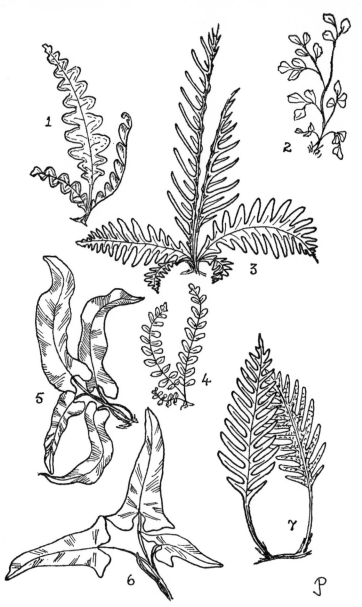

Figure 10   Rusty-back Fern *Ceterach officinarum*; 2 Wall Rue *Asplenium ruta-muraria*; 3 Hard Fern *Blechnum spicant*; 4 Spleenwort *Asplenium trichomanes*; 5 Hart's Tongue *Scolopendrium vulgare*; 6 *Scolopendrium hemionitis*; 7 Common Polypody *Polypodium vulgare*

vulgare) is only slightly less frequent on the peaks, but plentiful at lower altitudes. The hart's-tongue is only known from the summit of Puig de Massanella at over 4,100ft (1,250m), and possibly from a couple of other sites, while *Blechnum* is virtually confined to the slopes of Sierra del Teix.

Scolopendrium hemionitis, a close relative of the hart's-tongue, is widely distributed throughout the island in all suitable shady corners, and the common spleenwort (*Asplenium trichomanes*) and the shiny, deep green-black spleenwort (*A. adiantum-nigrum*) are very characteristic of intermediate elevations on the mountain slopes.

Colom attaches considerable importance to the distribution of bracken (*Pteridium aquilinum*) which occurs at elevations up to about 2,955ft (900m) from Galatzo north-eastwards to Formentor, since it roughly indicates the altitude of the 'Balearic' zone in the mountains, so important for the endemic flora. It is rather surprising to find a species so characteristic of acid soil growing at all in these predominantly limestone mountains. The brittle bladder fern (*Cystopteris fragilis*), occurring on the slopes of Puig Major and the Sierras del Teix, is a more northerly species much more typical of the lime-tolerant ferns.

CHAPTER FIVE

The insects

MAJORCA ABOUNDS IN insect life, and rarely a day passes without some interesting or unusual species being seen. Even in mid-winter, a host of brightly coloured beetles are about in the woods and shady ravines, while red admiral and speckled wood butterflies are tempted out of hiding by the numerous sunny, mild days. By March, a much greater variety of butterflies are to be seen, together with several of the more striking flies. May and June provide perhaps the greatest diversity of species: colourful beetles and bugs infest the flowers, while the plants of the waste ground and roadsides (notably thistles) are alive with a multitude of butterflies, mainly clouded yellows, meadow browns and various of the whites. Woodland glades and areas of maquis vegetation also hold numerous butterflies, mainly blues in variety, and the graceful sulphur-yellow Cleopatra, while damper ground and the pine-covered dunes provide favourite haunts of elegant dragonflies and damsel-flies of magnificent metallic sheen that glint in the sun as they swing to and fro along the rides, or hover helicopter-like among the reeds of the drainage canals. The marshes, dunes and streamsides also hold the large yellow and black swallowtail butterfly that flits and glides majestically over the vegetation, seeming so lethargic, yet surprisingly elusive on the wing. Bees, wasps and flies in infinite variety visit the flowers, including many large, exotic-looking forms, but the only ones that the visitor need fear are the familiar clegs, horse-flies and mosquitoes. At dusk, moths (including many of the large and spectacular hawkmoths) visit suburban gardens and street lamps, most particularly on close, thundery evenings, while a multitude of grasshoppers and crickets call throughout the day and night.

July and August are perhaps the poorest months, though grasshoppers are still plentiful, cicadas are in full song, and a number of butterflies continue to be seen though more typically on the higher ground now, since few flowers remain on the lowland where much of the vegetation is scorched and brown. Then with the advent of the autumn rains in September and October, and the unfolding of fresh vegetation, a new cycle begins: second broods of many of the spring species appear, together with the first broods of a number of casual immigrant butterflies and moths, that become considerably more plentiful at this season than during their first arrival in late spring. Many of these insects stay on the wing until near the end of the year, and consequently the visiting entomologist is assured of a good selection no matter what season of the year he chooses for his visit.

Some of the insect groups have been fairly thoroughly worked —notably the more conspicuous butterflies, moths and beetles, together with the dragonflies and damsel-flies, but others are as yet poorly known, and provide ample opportunity for the enthusiast to add to the existing rather fragmentary knowledge. In particular there is little information available on the ecological relationships between the various species of insects that inhabit the different specialised habitats that Majorca provides.

We are living in an age where man-made pollution is at last being seen, not just by the scientist, but increasingly by the man in the street, as a serious threat to the survival of many forms of life on this planet—not least to man himself. To an ever greater extent people are becoming aware of the rapidity with which changing environmental factors, including increasing land utilisation, can alter the balance of nature, and of the need to look closely at the likely future outcome of any proposed changes that might affect this balance. Where better to study such changes than in a rapidly developing, relatively isolated situation such as that provided by an island like Majorca, where conservation is so urgently needed, and where such a variety of life-form exist, many of which can already be seen to be engaged in the last desperate struggles for survival?

To give some idea of the scope that Majorca can still offer to the entomologist it is worth quoting some figures from the best represented and most thoroughly worked insect orders. Of the *Coleoptera* (beetles) some 2,000 species have already been listed, and it is probable that this figure represents little more than half of the true total, since more are being discovered regularly, many of which are endemic. The *Hymenoptera* (ants, bees and wasps) provide rather more than 300 species, of which rather fewer are endemic, but this is probably only a fraction of those actually present. The ecology, particularly of the parasitic species, is not at all well known and provides much scope for further work. *Lepidoptera*, being more conspicuous and more attractive from a collector's point of view, are better known, comprising at least 32 butterflies and some 250 of the larger moths, but even here the food-plants of a number of species are not known with any certainty in the Balearics. Of the *Diptera* (true flies) about 200 species have been described, and it is likely that this only scratches the surface of this large and difficult order. Lastly, the *Orthoptera* (grasshoppers and locusts) provide about 70 species. This latter order, together with the *Neuroptera* (ant-lions, lacewings, etc) and *Odonata* (dragonflies and damsel-flies) appears to be declining steadily throughout the Balearics—particularly in the latter cases, probably due to destruction of suitable habitats. Close study of all these orders would be well worth while: it is necessary to have a clear picture of their requirements for survival before any adequate steps towards their conservation can be taken.

The figures quoted here are in some cases quite accurate estimates of the present state of affairs in the various orders, but in others (and particularly in the case of some orders not mentioned, notably the *Hemiptera*—bugs) estimates merely serve to reveal the state of presentday ignorance. It must also be remembered that conditions change from year to year: even in such a well-known and intensively studied group as the birds, new species of a more migratory habit are being added to the list virtually every year, and a similar state of affairs will no doubt hold good on an even greater scale in the case of the less conspicuous insects. If the information given in this book stimulates naturalist readers to add only a handful of species to the lists, or, of greater importance, to be instrumental in saving even one of the gradually disappearing endemic varieties, then the writer will regard his task as having been well worth while.

Even as they stand, these figures represent very roughly some 10–20 per cent (depending on the particular order) of the totals for the whole of the Iberian Peninsula—yet the area occupied by all the Balearic Islands is only very close to 1 per cent of that of Spain and Portugal combined. This approximate comparison gives some idea of the disproportionate wealth of insect life to be found in the Balearics and, it is hoped, may serve further to emphasise the need to conserve the diversity of habitat necessary to ensure its survival within the islands—for in the world of the smaller forms of animal life minor variations in habitat or climate can wreak havoc not only among a relatively few species, but throughout the whole complex interplay of plant and animal associations that inhabit the particular ecosystem (as such associations, together with their containing environment, are known) that is at risk.

It is probably true to say that of all the various aspects of the natural history of an island, it is to the study of its insect population that one must turn in order to see most clearly the effects brought about by years of isolation from the mainland communities. To a large extent, this is a consequence of the fact that most insects have a very short life cycle, and that because of the very high mortality rate very large numbers are often involved in each generation. These factors combine to give a high potential for the appearance of new strains, since the chances of genetic modification are correspondingly higher than in other forms of life. Providing that the newly emerging strains prove to be competitive, and continue in isolation (as will be the case with the more sedentary species) new varieties can become established in a comparatively short period of time. Thus in Majorca we find a much greater selection of indigenous species and races as a proportion of the whole insect population than appears among the larger animals, or even the flowering plants.

New strains tend to arise most frequently among those species that have an inherent tendency towards variation, and polymorphism has been studied in a number of insect groups, particularly among some sedentary species, such as occur in the *Coleoptera* and *Hemiptera*. Indigenous species are less likely to arise among the more migratory forms, since continued immigration keeps the species in reproductive contact with the main lines of development of mainland communities, and there is correspondingly less opportunity for new strains to maintain the isolation necessary if they are to become established.

Finally in this introduction, it is necessary to apologise for the frequent use of Latin nomenclature when dealing particularly with the more local, southern European species and the various endemics, which have no English names. Throughout, the author has endeavoured to keep scientific names to a minimum, consistent with giving a balanced picture of the insect fauna likely to come to the notice of the visitor, together with the provision of an adequate skeletal account on which the more advanced entomologist can build.

It is most convenient to begin an account of the insects of Majorca with more or less detailed reference to the *Lepidoptera*, since in addition to the wealth of butterflies certain to attract the attention, this order provides one of the most migratory groups of insects, and thus the problem of insular subspeciation is not great. Furthermore, though little is as yet known about insect migration, what information is at present to hand refers largely to butterflies and moths, so that all in all these groups represent the best known of the Majorcan insect fauna.

LEPIDOPTERA

Butterflies

The resident population of butterflies is large and, considering the size of the island, remarkably varied, comprising in its 30 plus species a good 18 per cent of the total for all Iberia. In addition, numbers pass through the island on migration in most years and one or two species occur as casual vagrants. The large white, painted lady and queen of Spain fritillary are well-known trans-Mediterranean migrants, whose numbers in Majorca fluctuate from year to year, and whose appearance in coastal areas in spring often coincides with periods when landfall of migrant birds is taking place. This suggests not only that the butterflies are immigrants as well, but in addition that their appearance may be governed by similar conditions of wind and weather to those responsible for grounding the birds. On the face of it, this is a not unlikely conclusion, but much more work is required before it is substantiated, and it is in fields of inquiry such as this that the casual records of the holidaymaker can prove so valuable.

The red admiral and the long-tailed blue, though not uncommon during the spring months, usually show up more particularly on the return passage in autumn, but there is as yet no suggestion of any connection with bird migration at this season. There is, however, a slender but growing thread of evidence to suggest that strong WNW winds blowing from the Iberian Peninsula, or NE winds blowing from the Continent may be responsible for the appearance of mainland species as casual wind-drifted vagrants. The green hairstreak, for example, which does not as yet appear to be resident in the Balearics, has been noted directly following a period of strong NW winds that also brought griffon vultures and the first records for the Balearics of the white-rumped swift.

Many individuals from early broods of some of the resident butterflies are believed to emigrate northwards in spring. Insects on migration (as with the birds) tend to funnel up through the Formentor Peninsula on their way north, and from near the lighthouse of Cabo Formentor it is often possible to see thin streams of butterflies heading away from the coastline in a direction just east of north. Prominent in these movements are clouded yellows, various of the whites, and painted ladies, while the wall occurs rather more commonly in this arid area than elsewhere on the island up to an elevation of over 1,313ft (400m) during the spring months. Though suspicions may be strong, there is not yet any direct evidence for emigration of this latter species, however.

The butterfly population as a whole can conveniently be subdivided into three fairly distinct groups—those that are of widespread distribution throughout Europe, and as a consequence comprising the most adaptable (and often the most migratory) species; those more or less confined to a circum-Mediterranean or southern European distribution, but of fairly widespread occurrence throughout this range; and finally that group with a distinctly localised, disjointed distribution around the Mediterranean basin.

The numbers of the first group tend to fluctuate from year to year, depending on the extent to which they are reinforced by immigration, or depleted by emigration. This in turn is probably governed to some degree by prevailing weather conditions. Butterflies of the second group, usually of more sedentary habit, tend to be of more predictable appearance, though there is the point that a number of species of both classes show a preference for annual food plants, many of which enjoy only a brief growing season in spring, which can be adversely affected by a long dry spell. Species in the third group usually have very specialised habitat requirements, and can only continue to exist in those areas where their precise needs can be met: the very localised distribution that such species show is often an indication that they are heading towards eventual extinction. Fortunately, Majorca only possesses a single species in this latter class, though this probably indicates that a number of others in similar straits have already become extinct in the not too distant past.

However, it would not be difficult to draw attention to a
number of species of less exacting habitat requirements, whose
chances of survival are being prejudiced as a result of increasing
urbanisation. It may well only be a short while before they,
too, will have to be transferred to the relict list.

1 Butterflies showing a widespread Continental distribution

SWALLOWTAIL *Papilio machaon*. Found fairly commonly in lowland areas, particularly near the few permanent rivers and
stretches of marshland near which the favourite food-plant,
fennel, grows abundantly. It also strays to the sand dunes and
favours sheltered glades in the pinewoods. A magnificent insect
it cannot help but attract attention during April–July, while
another brood is on the wing about September–October.

SCARCE SWALLOWTAIL *Iphiclides podalirius*. True to its common
name, very much less plentiful than the previous species, particularly during the spring months, when it is in flight from
about May, usually in two broods, and appearing rather more
frequently later in the season. More typical of areas of richer
soil, notably around orchards where the larvae feed on the fruit
trees.

LARGE WHITE *Pieris brassicae*. Usually fairly plentiful in at least
two broods, but numbers tend to fluctuate from year to year.
Many individuals from the early broods appear to emigrate.

SMALL WHITE *Pieris rapae*. Abundant throughout spring and
summer in a variety of habitats. Occurs more frequently than
the previous species at higher elevations in the mountains, and
in areas of thinner garigue vegetation.

GREEN-VEINED WHITE *Pieris napi*. At times rather scarce in spring,
but becoming more plentiful as the season progresses, until one
of the more abundant species at the height of summer.

BATH WHITE *Pontia daplidice*. Appears later in spring than the
other whites—often not until the second half of May, though
still not uncommonly double-brooded. A large proportion of
the first brood is believed to emigrate (which may account for

its scarcity earlier in the year). Typically an insect of the richer garigue, waste ground and waysides.

CLOUDED YELLOW *Colias crocea*. Individuals that have over-wintered in hibernation are often on the wing in March, and by April–May the species is abundant throughout the island. It frequents wasteland where eggs are laid on vetches and other leguminous plants. The second brood of adults that follow in July–August are typically on the small side, possibly as a result of the rather dry climate of late spring. Numbers seem to emigrate in spring, and there is some slender evidence for a return passage in autumn.

Sampling has shown that the very pale female form *helice* (that could be mistaken for one of the larger whites at first glance) is rather more plentiful than in other populations, comprising about 25–30 per cent of all females from the early broods.

BRIMSTONE *Gonepteryx rhamni*. Rather uncommon in woodland glades and the richer maquis from early April, but may at times be overlooked in mistake for the female Cleopatra, though this species usually appears rather later. More plentiful in spring, and then irregularly throughout the summer. A number, particularly of the early broods, probably emigrate.

WOOD WHITE *Leptidea sinapsis*. Thinly but widely distributed in the richer maquis and open woodland, mainly on lowland areas and mountain foothills, April–October, usually in two broods.

CAMBERWELL BEAUTY *Nymphalis antiopa*. Very rare—a casual vagrant to the more elevated areas of thin woodland.

RED ADMIRAL *Vanessa atalanta*. May be encountered during mild spells throughout the winter, but hibernating individuals usually begin to make their appearance in April, while the species becomes more plentiful during May–July, with a further brood on the wing during September–December. Evidence for spring passage is at present slight, though some individuals probably emigrate, but numbers are swollen by return immigration in autumn.

PAINTED LADY *Vanessa cardui.* Likewise at least double brooded and distinctly migratory, but in contrast to the previous species is often more plentiful in spring than in autumn. Spring passage is regular, and part of the first brood probably emigrate, but autumn passage is somewhat variable, and needs more thorough investigation, though sometimes large numbers occur.

QUEEN OF SPAIN FRITILLARY *Issoria lathonia.* Appears on the wing early, sometimes in March, and in favourable years may have three broods. Rather local and erratic in occurrence, numbers being reinforced later in spring by trans-Mediterranean migrants, so that in some years the species can become almost plentiful, but this is the exception rather than the rule.

MEADOW BROWN *Maniola jurtina.* Of common occurrence in the more floriferous lowland areas from May, and in the *Ampelodesmus*/palmeto zone in the mountains rather later in June–July. The race concerned is *M. j. hispulla*, in which the female is particularly large and brightly coloured, with prominent 'eyes' on the forewings, and could easily be mistaken for a different species.

DUSKY MEADOW BROWN *Hyponephele lycaon.* The male of this species has recently been taken in the north-east of the island in June (following a period of strong NW winds), but the status of the species is probably no more than that of a casual wanderer: certainly breeding has not yet been verified. Other members of the grass-feeding *Satyridae*, notably of the genus *Erebia* (ringlets) are believed to occur on the coarse, thin grassland of the mountains, but the difficulty of the terrain makes their capture or certain identification difficult.

SMALL HEATH *Coenonympha pamphilus.* Fairly plentiful, mainly in upland areas of relatively poor vegetation, in a succession broods throughout the summer.

SPECKLED WOOD *Pararge aegeria.* In flight during March–July, and again during October–December, even appearing on mild sunny days in midwinter. Most plentiful in the spring months. Frequents open woodland, hedgerows and areas of richer maquis from sea level up to near the tree limit.

WALL *Lasiommata megera.* Usually double-brooded, March–June and again September–October, on wasteland, by roadsides, and in all grades of thin maquis and garigue. Quite common, even to 3,283ft (1,000m) in the mountains.

GREEN HAIRSTREAK *Callophrys rubi.* Has been noted on occasions, usually quite early in spring, on low ground and hillsides with thin maquis vegetation. At least some records coincide with periods of strong winds from the NE and WNW, so may be no more than a casual wanderer from the Continent.

LONG-TAILED BLUE *Lampides boeticus.* Appears in April, and thereafter intermittently until the end of the year in a succession of broods, usually thinly distributed but sometimes reinforced in spring by migrants. Many individuals from the early broods probably emigrate, while a distinct peak in autumn may be indicative of a return migration.

HOLLY BLUE *Celastrina argiolus.* Double-brooded from mid-April, more particularly in maquis and thin woodland, being greatly attracted to bramble blossom. Fairly widespread in suitable areas, and rather less frequently to near the upper limit of the tree zone at about 2,955ft (900m).

COMMON BLUE *Polyommatus icarus.* Abundant and widespread in cultivated areas, grassland, waste ground and thin woodland. On the wing from about mid-April, and frequently triple-brooded, specimens obtained in June–July being markedly smaller than those from spring and autumn broods.

SMALL COPPER *Lycaena phlaeas.* Flies almost throughout the year, though scarce in midwinter. Usually triple-brooded, and some individuals may hibernate for a short period in the cool season. Common and widespread in grassy areas and richer garigue, well up into the mountains.

MALLOW SKIPPER *Carcharodus alceae.* Thinly distributed in the *Ampelodesmus* grassland zone of the mountain slopes and the peaks of the Arta Peninsula—where other species may occur, but they are difficult to find in this rough terrain and are not at all well known.

1 Swallowtail *Papilio machaon*
2 Scarce Swallowtail *Iphiclides podalirius*
3 Cardinal *Pandoriana pandora*
4 Two-tailed pasha *Charaxes jasius*
5 Clouded yellow *Colias crocea* (a) male, (b) female, (c) var *helice*
6 Painted lady *Vanessa cardui*
7 Meadow brown *Maniola jurtina hispulla*
8 Cleopatra *Gonepteryx cleopatra*
9 Bath white *Pontia daplidice*
10 Mallow skipper *Carcharodus alceae*
11 Holly blue *Celastrina argiolus* (a) upper, (b) underside
12 Southern brown argus *Aricia cramera*
13 Lang's short-tailed blue *Syntarucus pirithous*
14 Assam silkmoth *Antheraea pernyi*
15 Spurge hawk moth *Celerio euphorbiae*
16 Striped hawk moth *Celerio livornica*
17 Hummingbird hawk moth *Macroglossa stellatarum*
18 *Truxalis nasuta*
19 Locust *Locusta migratoria*
20 Ant-lion *Ascalaphus ictericus*
21 Carpenter bee *Xylocopa violacea*

2 Butterflies with a southern European or circum-Mediterranean distribution

CLEOPATRA *Gonepteryx cleopatra*. Quite plentiful in thin woodland and maquis from about mid-April—these being individuals that have passed the winter in hibernation. Newly hatched butterflies are on the wing by the end of May, with a second brood in autumn.

TWO-TAILED PASHA *Charaxes jasius*. This large, exotic-looking

Page 108 (above) Shell of the endemic snail *Iberullus balearicus* from Puig Major—a particularly large example; (below) the Majorcan frog *Rana ridibunda* spp is particularly plentiful in the Gorg Blau

butterfly is an immigrant from North Africa, that first makes its appearance in May, and remains on the wing until about July, but only rarely in any numbers. The females lay their eggs on the strawberry tree (*Arbutus unedo*) that occurs not infrequently in shady valleys in the mountains, and along the wooded stretches of the east coast. Locally reared butterflies are in flight during September–October when the species becomes distinctly more plentiful.

CARDINAL *Pandoriana pandora*. Another immigrant from North Africa, though of vagrant status, this large, beautifully marked relative of the fritillaries may be encountered very occasionally in summer, usually on the mountain slopes where it may visit the flowering thistles.

STRIPED GRAYLING *Pseudotergumia fidia*. Uncommon, but may be met with occasionally on mountain slopes up to the tree line, more typically in late summer.

SOUTHERN GATEKEEPER *Pyronia cecilia*. Found among dry maquis and garigue from May onwards, but thinly distributed and difficult to locate. Probably double brooded, but little definite information.

FALSE ILEX HAIRSTREAK *Nordmannia esculi*. Sparsely distributed in grassy areas on the mountain slopes, principally in midsummer or later. Status uncertain, probably that of a vagrant that occasionally remains to breed: could be heading for the relict list.

LANG'S SHORT-TAILED BLUE *Syntarucus pirithous*. Quite common from early April throughout the summer in local concentrations amongst maquis and thin woodland notably at the foot of the Sierras. In some years can become abundant. The larvae feed on various species of broom that grow in the maquis.

SOUTHERN BROWN ARGUS *Aricia cramera*. Rather thinly, but generally distributed in garigue and grassy areas of lowlands and mountain foothills from May onwards, in a succession of broods, those of midsummer often giving distinctly smaller individuals than those of spring.

G

3 Butterflies with a disjointed Mediterranean distribution

MEDITERRANEAN SKIPPER *Gegenes nostrodamus*. Occasional in areas of thin grassland and garigue such as occur on the Arta Peninsula, from about May onwards.

In addition to the species listed above, other widely distributed members of the large family of *Satyridae* are believed to occur, and also probably the marbled white (*Melanargia galathea*), gatekeeper (*Pyronia tithonus*) and hermit (*Chazara briseis*) while of those species of a more restricted range, the black satyr (*Satyrus actaea*) has been suspected, but not yet obtained on the mountain slopes. There is undoubtedly scope for much further work on the butterflies of these mountainous areas, where the uneven rocky nature of the country and often shoulder-high clumps of coarse grass and palmeto make collection and identification an arduous and exhausting occupation.

Of the 175 or so species of butterflies found in the Iberian Peninsula, almost exactly half are of fairly widespread distribution throughout much of Europe, but in the case of the 32 species definitely recorded for the Balearics, no less than 23 are quite cosmopolitan, while of the remaining 9 at least a further 2 are believed to be reinforced by immigrant stock. Here we have striking confirmation of the general tenet that island populations contain a disproportionately large element of the more adaptable and more migratory species. On the other hand, we find in the case of the Mediterranean skipper and southern gatekeeper examples of more sedentary species that find in the thin garigue and rough grassland of the mountain slopes a habitat to which they are particularly well suited, and consequently can continue to survive without any need for modification of habit, though as this habitat gradually disappears there seems little doubt but that they must inevitably disappear with it.

Moths

Two day-flying moths are particularly plentiful throughout late

spring, and indeed for much of the year: these are the silver Y
or gamma (*Plusia gamma*) and the humming-bird hawk (*Macroglossa stellatarum*). Both of these species will be familiar to the
majority of British naturalists, but it is not often that we have
the opportunity of seeing the humming-bird hawk in such
profusion. In most years these delightful moths abound—particularly in the vicinity of honeysuckle, about which they love
to hover on whirring grey and gold wings while their long
proboscis seeks out the nectar from the base of the flower tube.
Numbers often resort to the floriferous gardens of the hotels
in the main holiday centres, where the visitors have been known
to mistake them for 'genuine' humming-birds! The insects are
equally plentiful around many of the mountain flowers, particularly the indigenous shrub of the St John's wort family,
Hypericum balearicum, which, when the blooms are beginning to
fade in late spring exude a very sweet-smelling nectar. They
occur quite commonly up to about 3,940ft (1,200m) in the
Sierras, and on top of the Arta mountains, where this shrub and
a variety of other flowers occur in profusion.

At dusk, a wide variety of other moths make their appearance,
principally during the period April–July and again following the
autumn rains. In spring they visit poppies and other flowers of
the fields and wasteland, and also honeysuckle, bouganvillea and
the various geraniums in the gardens of many of the villas and
hotels, so that quite a good selection can be obtained without
straying far from the outskirts of the main resorts (where the
street lighting also proves an added attraction). Here it is
only possible to select a few of the most striking of this large
group.

Of the *Sphingidae* or hawkmoths, perhaps the best represented
and most catholic in its tastes is the convolvulus hawk (*Sphinx
convolvuli*). Colom mentions that it is particularly fond of visiting the sand dunes in summer to feed from the large white
trumpets of the sea daffodil (*Pancratium maritimum*), but it is
also commonly found around honeysuckle, bramble and other
roadside flowers, and in gardens. During the day, it can often

be met with in ridiculously exposed situations, resting on walls, verandahs, and even on coconut-matting.

The equally large death's head hawk (*Acherontia atropos*), so named on account of the curiously shaped skull-like yellowish area on the thorax, flies at approximately the same seasons, May–July and September–November, though rather less commonly in the spring months. It shows a distinct preference for agricultural areas, however, where the larvae feed on the leaves of potato, at times doing considerable damage. Both larval and adult stages of this species are unusual in being capable of emitting quite a loud squeaking sound when handled.

The spurge hawk (*Celerio euphorbiae*) and the bedstraw hawk (*C. galii*) are both residents—the former quite common, but the latter distinctly less so. Neither of the adult insects are met with as frequently as their respective larvae, however. That of the spurge hawk in particular can be found fairly regularly in June and July feeding on a variety of spurges, perhaps most typically in coastal areas on the sea spurge (*Euphorbia paralias*). When fully grown, it is a magnificent animal, attaining a length of about 2½in (6cm), of greenish-black ground colour with a brilliant deep red stripe along the back that extends on to the curved horn on the last body segment, and large yellow and red patches on the flanks. The larva of the bedstraw hawk is a more sober shade of olive green, and has a row of yellow spots on either flank, which are outlined in black. This colour pattern makes it much less conspicuous among the spurges which form one of the favourite groups of food plants of this species also. It can, however, be located by careful searching on waste ground where the plants are frequent. Both these species are encountered most frequently after midsummer when adult, and it seems likely that numbers may emigrate northwards.

The striped hawk (*Celerio livornica*), another large and attractive sphingid, occurs, apparently as a resident, in fair, though rather variable numbers, and also on migration, but the equally beautiful silver-striped hawk (*Hippotion celerio*) is much less plentiful, being of uncertain appearance as an irregular migrant from Africa.

The large group of owlet moths (*Noctuidae*) is well represented and widespread throughout the island, but the identification of many of the species requires detailed knowledge, and is usually a matter for the specialist. Various of the brocades (*Trachea* spp and others) are known, and the abundant silver Y, one of the most migratory of all moths, also belongs to the *Noctuidae*, as does the much larger and very beautiful *Catacola deducta*, a close relative of the red underwing, that occurs not uncommonly in and about the oak woods, the leaves of which form the favourite food of the larvae.

The oak woods also harbour a number of members of the genus *Lymantria*, including the gypsy moth (*L. dispar*) and the closely related black arches (*L. monacha*), the larvae of which feed in compact groups on the bark of the trees, and may, on occasions, also attack fruit trees in some of the more elevated orchards. The larvae, fortunately, are preyed upon by a number of carnivorous beetles which congregate in the oak woods at the appropriate times of year.

In this same habitat occur rare individuals of the Assam silk-moth (*Antheraea pernyi*), which is very sparsely distributed in Europe, Majorca forming probably its most westerly station. Not being recognised as a particularly migratory species, the presence of this large tawny moth is believed by some authorities to provide a strong indication that the Balearics at some relatively recent period of their geological history were joined to the Eurasian landmass by a bridge to the eastward. There does not appear to be any evidence that the species could have been introduced.

The rather more widespread stands of stone pine provide a somewhat greater variety of species, prominent among which is the pine lappet (*Dendrolimus pini*) and many of the smaller varieties, including the pine beauty (*Panolis flammea*).

Waste places harbour a number of species associated with herbaceous foodplants, including various of the sharks (*Cucullia* spp), sword-grass (*Xylena* spp) and angle-shades (*Phlogophora meticulosa*). The silver Y flies by day and night in this habitat.

Processional moths of the genus *Thaumetopoeida* occur in both pine and oak woods, but particularly among the stands of pine-woods that back the coastal dunes. The larvae of these moths roam from one tree to another through the woods in a con-tinuous line often stretching for many yards. They frequently come to the attention of visitors sunbathing among the dunes, but one should beware of examining them too closely, as the long hairs on their backs can cause intense skin irritation; anyone who does handle these larvae should never rub their eyes after-wards.

Finally, another of the larger moths, the leopard moth (*Zeu-zera pyrina*), deserves mention on account of the damage that its larvae can cause in orchards. The adult has white wings dotted with blue-black spots, and the body reflects the same colour pattern, being bluish with narrow white rings. The female lays her eggs singly among newly opening leaf buds, and the young larvae enter the main stem and gnaw ascending galleries up through the branches. In more northerly latitudes the larvae take two full years to develop, hibernating twice in hollowed-out chambers, but in the mild Mediterranean winters hiberna-tion is not always necessary, and the growth period is often of shorter duration, so that the moth is on the wing at various seasons.

ORTHOPTERA

Grasshoppers, crickets, etc

Members of this order are widespread in areas of garigue, waste-land, mountain grassland and among the thin vegetation of the sand dunes during the spring months from April onwards. Of the short-horned grasshoppers, *Oedipoda gratiosa* is one of the most plentiful, particularly in grassy areas, throughout spring and summer, its brightly coloured hind wings briefly catching the sun in flight. Crickets chirp continuously during the afternoons and evenings, including a number of species of *Acheta* and *Gryllus*, domestic and field crickets. The mole cricket (*Gryllotalpa gryllotalpa*) which has exceptionally powerful forelegs and thorax does quite a lot of damage in gardens and among crops, destroying the roots of plants with its extensive burrowing activities. In contrast to this powerful, heavily built insect that looks more like a crustacean than a cricket must be mentioned the slender, delicate *Oecanthus pellucens* that reaches only about 1·5cm in length, and is of a curiously yellowish silky appearance, due to the presence of fine whitish hair on the body. This is a much more local species, confined to southerly latitudes in Europe, and occurs principally in the vineyards. It has a particularly sharp and penetrating chirp in the evenings, and generally appears rather late in the season.

Prominent in the group of long-horned grasshoppers is the great green grasshopper (*Tettigonia viridissima*), which is quite plentiful from late spring onwards. When disturbed from the herbage, it prefers to take to the air with strong fluttering flight. It chirps loudly from undergrowth by day, but contributes more particularly to the evening chorus of the balmy summer nights.

The strongly built greyish *Stauroderes bicolor*, together with *Chortippus pulvinatus* and reddish-brown *Gomphocerus* spp are more typical of the zone of *Ampelodesmus* grass and garigue, and occur high up in the mountains during the height of summer, when other lowland species are less vociferous. Other species of an essentially southern distribution include *Orthocanthacris aegyptis*, and the slender, delicate *Truxalis nasuta*, while *Parattetix meridionalis* still occurs in fair numbers around lagoons in the main areas of marshland, though tending to decrease as a result of the drainage operations. This same habitat holds large numbers of *Euprepocnemis plorans*, which is responsible for the monotonous, strident chirping that continues incessantly throughout all the marshes, day and night, from quite early in spring.

Dominant species of the pinewoods is the cicada (*Tettigia orni*), that sings persistently throughout the height of summer when many of the other crickets and grasshoppers have quietened down.

Relatively little is known about the migrations of the *Orthoptera*, with the notable exception, of course, of the locusts. *Locusta migratoria* does reach Majorca quite regularly in small numbers and it seems likely that the great green grasshopper is also immigrant, but little definite information is available.

DICTYOPTERA

Mantids

Majorca supports a good, but noticeably decreasing variety of mantids such as the praying mantis (*Mantis religiosa*) together with the closely related *Empusa agena*, *Iris oratoria* and members of the genus *Ameles*. They are carnivorous insects, found particularly in the north-east of the island among trees and the taller dune vegetation and also around the verges of marshland areas, where they lie in wait for their prey. In the early stages of growth this consists mainly of small flies, but later includes larger insects such as the larvae of various moths.

The praying mantis has a characteristic erect stance, with powerful forelegs held up in front of its face, waiting to pounce, that earns it its common name; when threatened it can assume most ferocious postures.

ODONATA

Dragonflies, damsel-flies, etc

This order contains some highly migratory insects and true to expectation we find that the Majorcan population is made up largely of the more widespread species. Without doubt, pride of place must go to the brilliant blue emperor dragonfly (*Anax imperator*), the wingspan of which can approach 5in (12cm). This magnificent insect can often be seen cruising majestically over pinewood glades along the dunes, and by the canals of the

Albufera. Other members of the group of larger hawker dragon-flies include representatives of the genus *Aeshna*, notably *A. squamata* of metallic bronze-green body colour. This and other species are normally on the wing from about mid-April or early May throughout much of the summer, but are by no means confined to an aqueous habitat apart from their mating and egg-laying activities. At other times they range freely over the whole island, being met with commonly in woodland glades at least up to 2,955ft (900m), and on the bare mountain tops of the Arta Peninsula, but their preferred habitat is probably the coastal sand dunes with their backing of thin pinewoods where they swarm during May–July.

Equally plentiful, and appearing about the same time of year, are the damsel-flies, notably the metallic-green *Lestes viridis* and the iridescent sky-blue *Coenagrion puella* though at all times these delicate insects are more closely associated with the areas of marshland, lagoons and slow-running streams where they breed. Distinctly scarcer, but not too uncommon as yet, are members of the genus *Sympetrum*, *S. fonscolombei* and *S. striolatum* being the most frequent, but others of this strongly migratory group turn up from time to time. In company with the dark reddish-brown-bodied *Crocothemis erythaea*, these latter species appear rather late in the season, not being generally on the wing until well into June. The lateness of their appearance may in the long run prove detrimental to their chances of survival, since in some years a particularly dry spring could result in mortality of the larvae as lagoons and other stretches of water begin to dry up.

Another species worthy of special mention in view of its markedly disjointed distribution is the graceful, dusky-bodied *Selysiothemis nigra*. Though locally not too uncommon in parts of its range, which extends from southern Europe into Asia, there are large, apparently suitable areas from which it has not been recorded. By no means a common Majorcan insect, it can nevertheless be seen during the summer months, often around woodland glades near the marshes. As it also appears late in the season, spring drought may be a limiting factor in this case, too.

Despite the considerable variety indicated here, there is no doubt that the *Odonata* as a whole are on the decrease in the Balearics, a distressing loss clearly attributable to the lack of fresh water on the island, which is being steadily aggravated by drainage of the few remaining areas of marshland.

NEUROPTERA

Lacewings and ant-lions

This order (also on the decline in the Balearics) derives its name from the criss-cross pattern of veins on the wings. It contains a number of interesting species, among which British visitors will recognise the familiar lacewing (*Chrysopa carnea*) and various of its relatives. The ant-lion (*Myrmeleon distinguendus*), superficially similar in the adult phase, is of interest from the point of view of the feeding habits of its larva. This insect digs shallow, loose-walled pits in the sandy areas on the dunes and fringes of woodland that are frequented by ants. The ants slide down the sides of the pit, whereupon the ant-lion larva uses its head to shovel down more loose sand on to the ants, preventing their escape until it is able to seize them in its strong pincer jaws.

Perhaps the most widespread of the *Neuroptera* in the Balearics, and certainly the one most likely to be encountered as it flies regularly by daytime throughout the spring and summer, is the rather vicious-looking *Ascalaphus ictericus*. Another member of the ant-lion family, the hairy-bodied adult with brown and yellow patterning of thin scales on its hindwings and long, club-tipped antennae hovers like a small dragonfly over fields near the marshes. In some areas it is still positively abundant.

COLEOPTERA

Beetles

This large and difficult order contains a good variety of species with a widespread European distribution, which continue to find adequate habitat requirements within the confines of Majorca. Many are to be found in the adult phase from about October through to early July, though numbers begin to decline steadily as the full heat of summer approaches. Others are dependent on the appearance of flowers, and are only commonly in view during the spring season. Water-loving species are active throughout the spring months, and again following the rainy season in autumn.

In addition to the remarkably large numbers of species of catholic distribution (which includes many of the chafers, flower beetles, ground beetles, dung beetles and longhorn beetles) there are also a considerable number whose range is restricted to an area that includes North Africa, Andalucia and other coastal areas of the Mediterranean basin. These include the slender, long-headed *Ophionea olivieri*, and the larger, violet-black *Oodes mauretanicus*, both fairly generally distributed in the Balearics. The large ground beetle *Campalita maderae* is of very restricted range in the extreme south-west of Europe, and its presence in Majorca clearly suggests the likelihood of the existence in former times of a land bridge uniting the Balearics with West Africa via Andalucia—as does the presence of the small brightly coloured flower beetle *Lachnaea paradoxa vicina*, that has a similar range, though this is a more mobile species, and therefore the possibility that it is a more recent immigrant cannot be completely ruled out. Members of other groups of a more sedentary nature show affinity with species of more localised distribution in the Aegean area, adding weight to arguments already noted in favour of a similar easterly bridge to the mainland.

Many of the *Coleoptera* are fairly rigidly confined to particular habitats—a consequence in the majority of cases of specialised and often very interesting life histories. As a result, it is most convenient in dealing with this order to consider the different habitats in turn, and outline the main varieties that they harbour.

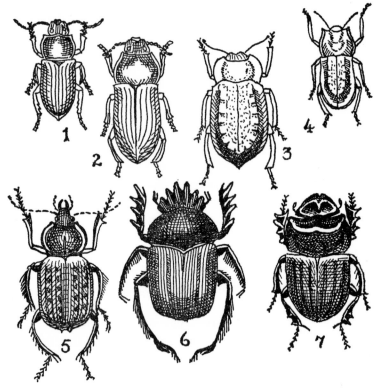

Figure 11   1 *Dendarus depressus*; 2 *Micrositus semicostatus*; 3 *Asida reichei*;
4 *Euryasida barceloi*; 5 *Calosoma sycophanta*; 6 *Scarabaeus sacer*;
7 *Copris hispanicus*

Ampelodesmus/thistle mountain zone

The insect life in general of this often very thinly vegetated area
is very restricted. Only a few small weevils of the genus *Sitona*
occur, feeding mainly on the vetches that straggle through the
coarse grasses, while the violet ground-beetle *Alphasida depressa*,
an endemic species of a genus of quite local southern European
distribution, can be found among debris on the drier slopes.
Other nocturnal ground beetles are fairly generally distributed
in this habitat and many of these are of great interest, since they

seem to be diversifying rapidly in this specialised habitat, having already thrown up a surprising number of endemic species and subspecies—usually a sign that the species-group concerned is in an active stage of evolution. This group, though at times difficult to find, should amply reward continuous close study.

The few flowering plants of this high zone harbour a small beetle population. The ubiquitous rose chafer (*Cetonia aurata*) destroys thistle heads in its search for nectar, while its larva attacks the roots of a variety of plants. The sea squill (*Scilla maritima*) harbours species of *Ditomus* and *Ophonus*, while the larvae of several species find its huge bulbs to their liking, including the curious ridge-backed *Brachycerus* spp which include a number of endemic species and forms.

Oak woods

The principal ground beetle of this habitat is the widespread and common *Calosoma sycophanta*, which in both larval and adult phases searches the trees for the larvae of various moths. Other notable species which spend much of the daylight hours among the debris brought down by the mountain torrents include *Bembidion genei*, and several members of the genus *Nebria*. Three species of longhorn beetles are known to inhabit the oak woods, these being the widespread *Cerambyx cerdo* and *C. scopolii*, together with the rather more local *C. mirbecki*. All these insects fly at dusk throughout the spring months, and lay their eggs on the bark of the oaks. The larvae feed at first on the inner layers of bark, later burrowing more deeply into the heartwood, where they may remain for two to three years before becoming fully grown.

Pinewoods

The characteristic longhorn of the pine trees is *Monohammus galloprovincialis*, which can become quite a pest in some years. It appears in May–June, along with a number of other species that attack the trees. These include the widespread bronze-green *Chalcophora mariana*, with characteristic furrowed wing cases, and the smaller but closely related *Buprestis octoguttata* and *B. nonnomaculata*, all of which devour the inner layers of bark in the larval stage. A variety of boring beetles also damage the pines, including *Apate monachus*, and the large brown chafer *Polyphylla fullo* with its distinctive fan-shaped antennae feeds on pine needles in June and July, while its grub is apt to attack the roots of the trees. The pinewoods also harbour the rare *Eurythyrea micans*, a tropical species with a magnificent metallic sheen to its upper surface, that has a very localised European distribution.

In the depths of winter, a variety of other local and endemic nocturnal species of the *Asidae* can be found in the woods, including *Euryasida barceloi*, *Insulasida moraquesi* and *I. planipennis*, that spend the daylight hours among debris, in the company of a variety of cockroaches, earwigs and centipedes. Most of these animals tend to retire well underground during the hot, dry months of summer.

Marshland

The stretches of marshland in the north-east of the island, the saltmarshes at Campos, and the few permanent, slow-flowing watercourses that persist throughout the year harbour a rich fauna of hygrophilic beetles. These mostly make their appearance in early February, and remain active during the spring months, disappearing in the heat of summer, only to reappear again with the advent of the autumn rains. They spend much of their time in galleries among the roots of rushes and sedges, and are in general imperfectly known. Colom lists members of the genera *Bembidion*, *Chlaenius*, *Amblistoma*, *Pogonus*, *Tachys*, *Apotomus*, *Agonum*, *Calathus*, *Zuphium*, *Panagaeus*, *Drypta*, *Brachinus*, *Oodes*, *Ophionea* and *Pterostichus* as being particularly well represented, including a number of local and endemic species—a ripe field here for more careful study.

Aquatic carnivorous species of the family *Dytiscidae* are abundant. Many are good divers, catching their prey under water, and are quite strong fliers, being airborne usually by about dusk. In this group, members of the genera *Agabus, Meladema, Cybister, Dytiscus* and many others are known, while whirligig beetles of the genus *Gyrinus* spiral and tumble in more open water among the reeds.

Scavenging water beetles belonging to the genus *Hydrophilus* are well represented in stagnant water. The carnivorous larvae hatch from egg-masses laid in watertight floating cocoons spun by the female. Adults of this genus are quite actively on the wing at night, and can be taken at lights.

Sandy beaches and dunes

Many of the dune beetles are nocturnal, spending the daytime in subterranean galleries, but of those that can be encountered in daylight, various of the ridged *Brachycerus* species also found at higher levels occur, and so does the predatory *Eurynebria complanata*. The large, dark red-brown *Carabus morbillosus*, though occurring in a variety of habitats, seems particularly attracted to the dunes, as do a number of other members of the *Carabidae*. This is probably on account of the multitude of snails that congregate in coastal areas, particularly during the spring months. Several of the larger *Carabidae* have a long, narrow head and thorax which enables them, having once bitten a snail, to retain their hold and be drawn in after it, as the snail attempts to retreat into its shell. Larvae of the shark and sword-grass moths are also taken.

Other nocturnal beetles particularly abundant on the drier dunes include members of the genera *Pimelia, Pachychila, Stenopsis* and *Scaurus*. Many of these families are peculiar to dry, sandy habitats, and some are of restricted circum-Mediterranean distribution. In Majorca, a number of local races and species have evolved. Many of the genus *Pimelia* in particular have well-developed bristly hairs on their legs, while those of *Scaurus*

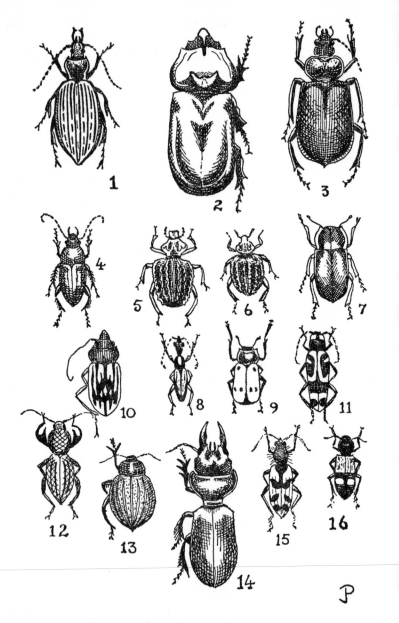

Figure 12   1 *Carabus morbillosus*; 2 *Oryctes nasicornis*; 3 *Campalita maderae*; 4 *Oodes mauritanicus*; 5 *Brachyserus barbarus*; 6 *Brachyserus balearicus*; 7 *Alphasida depressa*; 8 *Ophionea olivieri*; 9 *Lachnaea paradoxa*; 10 *Eurynebria complanata*; 11 *Xylotrechus arvicola*; 12 *Scaurus rugulosus*; 13 *Pimelia cribra*; 14 *Scarites gigas*; 15 *Trichodes umbellatarum*; 16 *Tillus transversalis*

Page 125 A pair of black-winged stilts *Himantopus himantopus*

Page 126 Kentish plover *Charadrium alexandrinus* covering eggs

have spade-like processes on the forelegs: both these features are of great assistance in digging into loose sand, the beetles often rolling from side to side, in order to make full use of all three legs on each flank at a time.

On the sandy verges of the pinewoods backing the dunes, the carnivorous larvae of various tiger beetles lie in wait for their insect prey at the mouth of subterranean tunnels. The widespread *Cicindela campestris*, which occurs in the Balearics in a variety of colour forms, is probably the commonest, but *C. flexuosa*, *C. lunulata* and *C. germanica* are also known. At dusk, the ferocious-looking carnivorous *Scarites gigas* often ventures out of the pinewoods to prey on the smaller insects that feed among the low dune plants.

Agricultural zone

In grain fields occurs the widespread *Zabrus tenebrioides*, the larvae of which feed on young leaves of the various cereal crops in spring, together with beetles of the genus *Carterus*. A variety of species occur in the orchards, where they can prove to be even more destructive: these include the elegant *Xylotrechus arvicola*, *Acanthoderes clavipes*, and various members of *Clytanthus*. Numbers of carabid beetles act as general scavengers among the vegetable detritus, including *Scarites* spp, while from late May onwards a variety of dung beetles remove the excrement of grazing animals from the areas of poorer grassland. Noteworthy in this latter group is *Scarabaeus sacer*, the sacred scarab of the ancient Egyptians.

During June and July, *Oryctes nasicornis* is likely to attract attention in view of the strong, curved, rhinoceros-like horn that projects from the top of its head. The adults are general scavengers on waste and agricultural land, but the larvae are found more particularly in oak woods. The characteristically elliptical *Copris hispanicus* becomes widely distributed, though not yet over-plentiful, at this season, reappearing more abundantly after the autumn rains.

H

Dry garigue

This habitat supports few species, but those that are present are quite interesting, including many of the endemic ground beetles also encountered in the mountains. As the majority are nocturnal, they require careful searching for. Other endemics occur right through the height of summer, when the majority of beetles are much less conspicuous: these include *Microsetus semicostatus curtulus*, *Phylan abbreviatus* and various *Dendaurus* spp.

Foliage and flower beetles of the wayside and waste ground

A number of smaller, brightly coloured beetles are dependent upon the flowering of a variety of wayside plants for their appearance. Species of the family *Oedemeridae* occur abundantly in wide variety, while *Tillus transversalis* frequent thistles and *Trichodes umbellatum*, as its specific name implies, infests umbelliferous plants. *Tropinota squalida* and *Oxythyrea funesta* join the related rose chafer (*Cetonia aurata*) in destroying the flowerheads of a variety of plants, but most particularly the thistles, daisies and marigolds.

Other beetles depend on the opening of flowers for a different reason. The parasitic larvae of the oil beetles, *Melöe rugosus*, *M. tuccius* and *M. proscarabaeus* lie in wait among flowerheads until they are visited by bees. The larvae snatch a free ride by attaching themselves to the hair of bees, being thus transported to their nests. Here the larvae drop off into the nest, where they feed avidly on the food stored by the bees until fully grown, eventually leaving the nest to pupate.

Likewise closely associated with herbaceous plants are a wide variety of leaf beetles. The following are generally abundant in late spring, *Lachnaea paradoxa* and *Podagria fuscicornis* on various of the mallows, and *Chrysomela* spp. The interesting endemic *Timarcha balearica*, a polymorphic species known locally as 'escarabat de sang' (blood beetle) is widespread throughout the spring, and the ladybird *Coccinella septempunctata* swarms on herbaceous plants in May and June. This latter species, together with the rather less abundant *C. decimpunctata, Epilachna chrysomelina* and *Adalia bimaculata* are widespread in the Balearics, and are probably at least partially migratory.

Bees, wasps, etc

Reaching another of the stronger flying orders, we again find that the more widespread Continental members are well represented in Majorca. The carpenter or black bee (*Xylocopa violacea*), at first glance more like a large black beetle in flight, is quite plentiful among those of a more southerly distribution, and there are a number of more local species of solitary bees (*Podaliridae*) and an interesting variety of parasitic species.

The seasonal cycle begins as early as February, when the solitary bee *Podalirius acervorum* first appears on the wing. By the following month, the larger *P. nigrocinctus* is about, together with a number of closely related species including the endemic *P. balearicus* of dark thorax, the abdomen relieved by narrow yellowish bands, and the uniformly brownish *Eucera numida*. Other solitary bees include the ground nesting *Andrena flessae*, which appears in April, followed in May and June by others of the same genus.

By this time of year, numbers of other mining bees have appeared, including *Halictus, Colletes* and several species of *Osmia*. In addition to excavating nests in the usual sandy slopes, these bees are always ready to improvise, and will readily appropriate the old galleries of the larvae of beetles that are exposed in the bundles of cut reeds left at the sides of the drainage canals in the marshes: they will also at times use holes excavated by the larvae of wood-boring species.

The red-and-black mason bee (*Chalicodoma sicula*) also appears at the same season, but the leaf-cutters, including the common leaf-cutter (*Megachile centuncularis*), are not plentiful until late June or July. When these and the other bees are well on

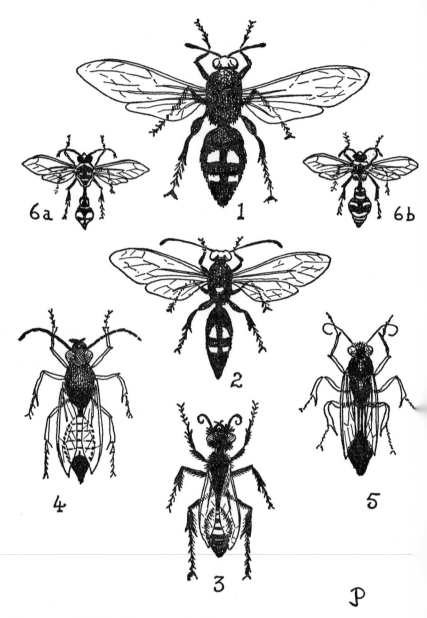

Figure 13 1 *Scolia flavifrons*; 2 *Scolia bidens*; 3 *Ammophila hirsuta*; 4 *Sphex maxillosus*; 5 *Sceliphra spiriphex*; 6a and b *Eumenes coarctatus* ssp

the wing, the parasitic species appear. *Melecta luctuosa albovaria* and *Crocisa major* are two well-distributed members of this group that invade the nests of other bees and lay their eggs therein. Other insects parasitic on bumble bees in particular include several members of the family of velvet ants (*Mutilla* spp), bee-like insects generally recognisable by the red-brown thorax which contrasts sharply with the dark abdomen.

Turning to other members of the *Hymenoptera*, we find the wasps *Ellis ciliata*, *Scolia bidens* and *S. flavifrons*—the two latter being particularly large, vicious-looking creatures. These are parasitic on various beetles, depositing their eggs beneath the skin of the larvae. As the species attacked are mostly boring beetles that are pests in orchards, the attentions of these wasps is by no means unwelcome.

The most plentiful of the social wasps is the German wasp (*Vespa germanica*), which constructs massive paper nests containing thousands of individual cells, in underground chambers that it excavates. The smaller *Polistes gallicus*, of more tapering body, is also widespread, constructing flattish, disc-like nests in low herbage and between stones. Heath potter wasps (*Eumenes coarctata*) occur in a number of local forms: they capture the larvae of geometer moths, take them into the nest, and there deposit their eggs, sealing the nest afterwards. When the eggs hatch, the young larvae have a ready-made food supply.

The mason wasps are well represented on the island, with *Odynerus danctici*, *O. simplex* and *O. parietinus*, and the sand dunes support a good variety of sand wasps including *Sphex maxillosus* and the widespread red-banded sand wasp (*Ammophila sabulosa*) together with other *Ammophila* spp. The large *Scolia bidens* and *S. flavifrons*, already mentioned, also occur most commonly along the coastline, among the pine-fringed dunes, while ants in variety abound in this habitat, and by the marshes and woods.

OTHER INSECT ORDERS

In the *Diptera* (flies), those most likely to attract the attention are the *Syrphidae* (hover-flies), which include some large bee-like species, such as the handsome but intimidating *Volucella zonaria*. This species is parasitic on a number of bees, entering the nests often forcibly, to deposit its eggs, the larvae scavenging in the nests until ready to pupate. Members of the slightly smaller yellow-and-black genera *Syrphus* and *Helophilus* are well represented.

The presence of multitudes of mosquitoes, gnats and midges is more likely to be a cause of intense irritation (both metaphorically and physically) rather than a matter of enthusiasm for the amateur, but attention must again be drawn here to their value as a food supply for early migrant birds that frequent the marshes in huge numbers in spring—particularly in bad weather, when other food is in short supply.

Hemiptera (bugs) are well represented in a variety of habitats. Aquatic forms are particularly plentiful, including the awkward, secretive water scorpion (*Nepa cinerea*), and the widespread, familiar water boatman (*Notonecta glauca*), together with a variety of pond skaters (*Gerridae*) and water crickets (*Veliidae*). By far the most brightly coloured are the shield bugs, flower- and leaf-dwelling species of which the island supports a good selection, notably of the genera *Eurydemas*, *Graphosoma* and *Calocoris*, that are generally typical of southern Europe, but also various local forms that have not yet been fully described—as would be expected in a more sedentary group of insects such as these.

CHAPTER SIX

Other invertebrates

OF THE REMAINING orders of invertebrates yet to be considered, there is no doubt that the shell-bearing molluscs have attracted the most attention. The calcium content of the sedimentary surface rocks of Majorca is very high, and being in a fairly soluble form in several areas provides an abundant supply of lime, the essential mineral for shell construction; additionally the terrain is in the main ideally suited to the land-based molluscs.

Despite the shortage of fresh water on the island, the few slow-running permanent watercourses and the less saline areas of marshland have an alkaline reaction, and a very high content of dissolved calcium. They support a large concentration of fresh-water molluscs, including the widespread great pond snail (*Limnaea stagnalis*) which as its specific name suggests, is found almost exclusively in stagnant water. The marsh snail (*Limnaea palustris*) together with other species of the same genus occur also in the slower-flowing stretches of the watercourses, as do various of the *Planorbidae* (ramshorn snails)—a group that includes one or two endemic species.

Among the fresh-water crustaceans, we can also find a number of interesting cases of insular subspeciation. The fresh-water shrimp *Gammarus pungens* is of very local distribution around mainly the littoral belt of the western Mediterranean basin, and gives rise to endemic forms in both Majorca and Minorca. (In passing, it is of interest to note that the corresponding shrimp of Ibiza has a much closer affinity with a species commonly found in North Africa, *G. klaptoczi*, which poses the rather unlikely possibility that Ibiza might have been in direct overland contact

133

with the African mainland *after* the land bridge between Majorca and Ibiza had submerged!)

Another amphipod peculiar to Majorca is *Porrasia mallorquinensis*, found in a restricted locality of more saline water near Santa Ponsa. The fairly widespread small waterlouse *Jaëra balearica* is another quite distinct endemic species, more characteristic of stretches of fresh water, where also occurs a variety of leeches as yet not well known, but including *Herpobdella testacea*.

Returning to the molluscs, it is the terrestrial group of the class *Gastropoda* that has attracted the most attention to date. This is probably the direct result of at least three main factors. In the first place, the group as a whole is very sedentary in nature by comparison with other forms of animal life. It is thus quite possible for the population of one particular area to be completely isolated from a neighbouring population as little as $\frac{1}{2}$ or 1 mile (1 or 2km) away, and as we have already noted, reproductive isolation is one of the most important factors in leading to the development and stabilisation of local races, and eventually to the production of entirely distinct species. Further, as many of the species are polymorphic, there is ample scope for the ecologist to study the survival value of the various colour and pattern forms in different surroundings. In the arid, mountainous areas, for example, snails form one of the staple items in the diet of the blue rock thrush, and it is interesting to see how the ground colour of the shells of the snails taken by these birds varies from area to area, but more particularly to note the seasonal variation in colour for the shells from one particular area, suggesting that different colour forms have different survival value as the background colour of the vegetation changes.

Thirdly, the molluscs as a whole have attracted a lot of attention from geologists, as shell-backed creatures in general tend to leave one of the most complete and easily traceable fossil records. Such fossils occur abundantly in the Quaternary deposits found more particularly in the south of the island, and in the large bays of the south-west and north-east coasts, and have been used to trace the stages in the gradual extinction of various relict species and groups, and the emergence and diversification of others. Colom and other authors have treated this aspect of the natural history of the molluscs in some detail.

The gastropods contain a number of species of quite widespread distribution in Europe, that find conditions to their liking, and show little deviation from the mainland stock, notable among which are the grove snail (*Cepaea nemoralis*) and a number of others, including *Bythinia leachei*, *Pyramidula rupestris* and *Punctum pygmaeum*. Much more typical of the island, however, is a variety of species more essentially restricted to a southern European or Mediterranean distribution. Of these, the best known include *Archelix punctata*, *Eobania vermiculata*, *Euparypha pisana*, *Granopupa granum*, *Melanopsis dufouri* and several others. Most of this group are typical of the drier areas of porous limestone, the first two in particular being very widespread, and ascending to the summit region of the higher mountain peaks in the Sierras. By contrast, *Euparypha pisana* tends to prefer areas supporting a rather richer vegetation. In late spring and summer it collects by thousands on herbaceous plants of the waste ground and sand dunes, particularly in the Bays of Alcudia and Pollensa, where it attracts numbers of the predatory carabid ground beetles.

Coming in turn to molluscs of a rather more localised distribution, Colom cites as a typical example *Pseudotachaea splendida*, confined on the mainland to the maritime levantine provinces of Spain and southern France, and in Majorca alone of the Balearics. *Fruticicula lanuginosa* and *Leucochroa cariosula* are two species of even greater interest in that their present known range is even more restricted: outside the Balearics, they are found only in north Morocco, and the extreme south-west of Spain.

The genus *Iberillus*, characterised by the beautifully marbled patterning on the shells, provides perhaps the most extreme example. Known from fossil remains to have been in existence since at least the Quaternary era, *Iberillus* is virtually confined, apart from a couple of small mainland colonies, to the Balearics. Here, however, it exists in a number of local, clearly defined

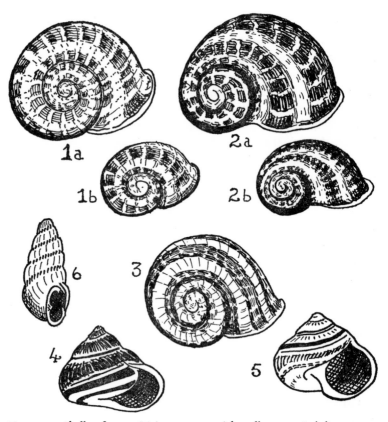

Figure 14   Shells of some Majorcan terrestrial molluscs: 1 *Archelix punctata* (a) mountain form, (b) lowland form; 2 *Helix aspersus* (a) and (b) as above; 3 *Eobania vermiculata*; 4 *Pseudotachaea splendida*; 5 *Euparypha pisana*; 6 *Rupestrella moraguesi*

species, within which are several even more localised, true-breeding forms. *Rupestrella moraguesi*, a fairly plentiful inhabitant of the north-west Sierras deserves mention in passing, in that it suggests the possibility of a former connection with the Tyrrhenian Islands, where the genus of which it is the most westerly representative is well represented.

A further aspect of the natural history of the molluscs that has attracted quite a lot of attention is the phenomenon of gigantism. Populations of a number of species, but notably of *Iberellus balearicus*, *Archelix punctata* and *Helix aspersa* consistently reach a much greater size than normal, at elevations from about 3,283ft (1,000m) upwards in the north-west Sierras, most particularly in the vicinity of Puig Major. This tendency towards gigantism is a characteristic of the whole population, and is often sharply differentiated from neighbouring populations at only slightly lower altitudes. The reason for this phenomenon is not yet fully understood, but as the zone of demarcation roughly corresponds with the summer cloudbase level, it seems likely to be closely related to the much greater humidity that will prevail above this level. This may have the effect of considerably shortening, or even eliminating altogether the need for a period of dormancy, in which many lowland snails pass the time of summer drought, and thus permitting a longer growing season each year. Be that as it may, the difference in neighbouring populations is often quite remarkable, in some cases increasing overall measurements by more than 10 per cent.

Finally in this chapter, brief mention of one of the least studied, but nevertheless one of the best represented classes of invertebrates on the islands, the *Arachnida* (spiders). Members of this class become most prominent in late spring and summer, with species of the genus *Araneus* and *Epeira* spinning webs in the vicinity of the few remaining stretches of water, in order to trap the insects that congregate there at the onset of the summer drought. Large species of wolf spiders of the genus *Lycosa* lie concealed awaiting the opportunity to spring out on their unsuspecting prey, while members of the closely related *Tarantula* (harmless to humans in the European forms) are believed to occur, but spend much of their time in hiding, and are consequently difficult to find.

CHAPTER SEVEN

Amphibians and reptiles

MOST OF THE southern European amphibians revel in the sunny, but yet not too dry Mediterranean climate, and there is no doubt that it is only the extreme shortage of surface water during the long summer season that restricts the spread of this group of animals in Majorca. As it is, every available watercourse and damp ditch holds its population—everywhere that moisture sufficient for their needs can be found. To an even greater extent the lowland marshes of the Albufera of Alcudia and the smaller Albufereta near Pollensa swarm with frogs, together with smaller numbers of toads, which occur more frequently further away from water. They croak, purr and trill continuously throughout the day and night, accompanying the crickets and cicadas that tune up at dusk in a massed twilight choral performance that carries far on the still air of the calm Majorcan evenings.

The typical frog of the island is the local form of the marsh frog (*Rana ridibunda*) which has a rather interesting distribution on the mainland. The nominate race is essentially of Eurasian origin, and does not extend westwards much beyond the Aegean, except in a few areas such as the British Isles, where it has been introduced. Another race, *R. r. perezi*, occurs quite commonly throughout much of North Africa, from whence it is believed to have spread northwards into the Iberian Peninsula where it is now widespread. It is this latter race that the Majorcan frog most resembles. Measuring some 5–6in (12–14cm) long, it comes intermediate in size between the edible frog (*Rana esculenta*), typical of south-central Europe and averaging 3·1–4·7in (8–12cm), and the distinctly larger eastern race of the marsh frog, that can exceed 6in (15cm). Though variable in appearance, it normally lacks the pale dorsal stripe shown by most edible frogs, and has the more warty skin and rather longer snout characteristic of *ridibunda*. Yet on the mainland, *ridibunda* is known as an essentially lowland species, whereas in Majorca these frogs occur at least to above the 2,626ft (800m) level in the mountains: visitors to the Gorg Blau, which still retains a very humid atmosphere even in the height of summer, can disturb basking frogs at almost every step.

The main food supply of the frogs comprise fresh-water shrimps, water-boatmen and dragonfly larvae, but they are also cannibalistic devouring the young of their own species—a characteristic typical of *ridibunda*. This prompts the suggestion that both the edible and marsh frog formerly inhabited the Balearics (the former still occurring in the Tyrrhenian Islands), possibly even interbreeding, but that the latter has gradually driven out the smaller edible frog. In support of this idea, it is worth noting that introduction of the marsh frog into the southern counties of the British Isles has resulted in a marked decrease in numbers of other species.

The green tree frog, a much smaller species that can vary greatly in colour according to situation and humidity, is most vociferous at night, with a sharper, more penetrating, almost yelping croak. It climbs well, and often takes flying insects. In distribution, it tends to be restricted to the main areas of marshland, though becoming more widespread in the damper months of spring and autumn.

The toads are represented in the Balearics by three species, the green toad (*Bufo viridis*), the natterjack (*B. calamita*) and the midwife toad (*Alytes obstetricans*). The green toad purrs monotonously all day long in the marshes, and often continues well into the night, when it is most active, but it can be seen by day especially following thunderstorms that occur not infrequently on summer afternoons. The natterjack is much more strictly nocturnal, and consequently very difficult to locate, except by call. It is most vociferous during the late spring months, but seems very thinly distributed, mainly around the sandy bays near the marshes in the north-east of the island. Its exact status is little known, and records are few.

In contrast to the fairly cosmopolitan natterjack, and the more easterly origin of the green toad, the final species, the midwife toad, is more essentially restricted to a south-westerly distribution in Europe. This species derives its name from its peculiar breeding habits. In late spring, the male carries long strings of eggs twined around its hind legs until just before they are due to hatch, when they are shed into water. It inhabits both low-land marshes and damp areas in the mountains, and has a most surprising ringing call, not at all reminiscent of a toad, but more like that of a bird—loud, clear and quite musical.

Most of the frogs and toads, particularly those of more southerly distribution, do not take kindly to temperatures below about 44-6° F (7-8° C), and tend to hibernate intermittently from mid-December until early March, reappearing again during spells of warmer weather in midwinter. Perhaps the most confirmed hibernator is the green tree frog, that becomes noticeably scarcer after the end of October, and does not become really plentiful again until late March. It is noteworthy that the newts, typically of more cool temperate distribution, do not appear to have been recorded in Majorca.

The aquatic terrapin (*Emys orbicularis*) has been recorded on occasion from the marshes in the north-east of the island, where it may be met with sunning itself on sandy stretches at the water's edge, usually during the late spring. Though generally lethargic by day, particularly during the heat of summer, it becomes quite active at night, and swims energetically and well. When fully grown, it can approach 11½in (30cm) or so in length (including the tail). It has not yet been recorded from Campos, nor from the marshes near Magaluf, in the south-west. The land tortoise *Testudo hermanni* that inhabits the drier areas of garigue vegetation is less well known. It spends most of the long dry summer in a state of dormancy, often half buried, and is only at all active for a few months in spring and summer, being then mainly nocturnal. Both these species tend to go into partial hibernation during the colder spells in the winter months, usually from about late October to February or March. The terrapin feeds on insects and molluscs and is sufficiently active in the water to be able to take small fish; the tortoise is entirely vegetarian. Both lay their eggs in the soil late in the spring and, following incubation by the summer sun, these hatch with the coming of the rainy season in autumn.

Four species of snake inhabit the Balearics, but the present status and distribution of two of these is very imperfectly known. The grass snake (*Natrix natrix*) is fairly well represented, mainly in the lowland areas and humid, shady sites that support more lush vegetation. In its favourite haunt, the marshy verges of the Albufera and Albufereta, it not infrequently attains a great size—not far short of 7ft (2m) in extreme cases. The viperine snake (*Natrix maura*), which has a back pattern superficially similar to the British adder or viper, but can be distinguished by the row of white or pale yellow spots on either flank, is typically even more restricted to an aqueous habitat, and occurs principally on the same two stretches of marshland, where both prey on frogs, toads, fish, worms and insects.

The ladder snake (*Elaphe scalaris*) is known to inhabit Minorca, and probably also still occurs in Majorca. It is of rather localised distribution around the shores of the western Mediterranean, and prefers a drier habitat, frequenting orchards and vineyards in particular. It preys on mice, and probably also on the geckos that live in the walls of these drier areas. The final species, the cowl snake (*Macroprotodon cucullatus*), is known to occur in Majorca, but as it is essentially a nocturnal reptile, there is little definite information on its abundance. It seems likely to be fairly scarce, however, mainly in the drier areas. In appearance, it is not unlike the European smooth snake, though rather warmer, sandy-brown on the upperparts. All four species are harmless to man.

During the winter months, all the snakes go into hibernation for varying periods, usually from about the end of October until

April. *M. cucullatus* is the earliest to reappear in spring—often before the end of March, which is surprising as it is a species of essentially southerly latitudes, and *Elaphe scalaris* (of closely similar distribution) is usually the last to appear, often not until early May. If the summer should prove to be particularly long and dry, a period of dormancy may ensue, but in any case all four species become distinctly less active during the hot season.

Of the broad-toed lizards or geckos, two species are quite widely distributed throughout the Balearics. The wall gecko (*Tarentola mauretanica*) is the more abundant in lowland areas, among rocky stretches of garigue and more particularly on walls and around buildings, where it can often be seen sunning itself by day. A cautious approach is required, however, for at the slightest disturbance it vanishes into cracks in the walls. When fully grown, it is slightly larger and more uniformly coloured than the other resident species, the disc-fingered gecko (*Hemidactylus turcicus*), though the colouring of both is very variable, and dependent on the surroundings. The latter species often has dark mottling on the upperparts, and a series of dark bars is usually prominent across the otherwise pale tail. It is not infrequent in the mountains, but also occurs in the lowlands, where it often enters buildings, being much bolder in its habits than the wall gecko. Both species are favourite items in the diet of the ubiquitous hoopoe.

The true lizards of the Balearics belong to the group of wall lizards, and have attracted scientific interest on account of their great tendency towards diversification and polymorphism. They evidently originated in the main from Spanish stock, showing close affinity to the levantine race of the Iberian species *Lacerta bocagei*. When the Balearics followed the Pityusens into separation from the mainland of the Iberian Peninsula towards the end of the Tertiary, a series of endemic races gradually developed, giving rise to the species-groups *L. lilfordi* and *L. pityusensis* respectively. Both groups show distinct common characters which warrant more than subspecific status, yet each group shows great variability within its members. These, together

Page 143 Booted eagle *Hieraaetus pennatus* on nest

Page 144 (above left) Black vulture *Aegypius monachus*; (above right) Bonelli's eagle
Hieraaetus fasciatus; (below left) Eleanora's falcon *Falco eleanorae*; (below right) thekla lark
Galerida theklae

with the endemic molluscs already mentioned, form perhaps the best studied group of Balearic fauna. Colom details the various forms, listing no less than 35 distinct races of *L. piyusensis*, and in Majorca and Cabrera 8 races of *L. lilfordi*, with another 7 occurring in Minorca.

Reverting more particularly to the Majorcan population, the most surprising fact is that the wall lizard is not at all common on the mainland itself, being more or less restricted to the Quaternary deposits of the south-east coast. The main population occurs on the various groups of small offshore islets stretching around the south coast from Dragonera in the west to Caragol, and the more distant Cabrera group in the extreme south. These islets are believed to have separated from the mainland at various periods fairly early in the Quaternary, and each small cluster carries its own true-breeding endemic population. One or two races are varying shades of sandy- or grey-brown in colour, blending well with the general background, and of obvious protective advantage, but most are of a much darker shade, in many cases being nearly completely black. This tendency towards melanism is often found in island populations, and is not yet fully understood. It may be connected with restriction in feeding habits, but seems more likely to be a response to climatic factors, perhaps connected with temperature regulation. There is also some evidence for a correlation between the incidence of melanism and a trend towards relict status, which the case of the Majorcan lizards tends to be confirmed in that the more melanistic forms are usually found on the islands that are believed to have been separated from the mainland for the greatest period of geological time. This is a field in which active research is in progress, and even casual observations are of value.

The general restriction of the lizards to the more southerly part of the Majorcan group of islands is not surprising in the case of these sun-loving reptiles. Hence the relatively recent discovery of another race on the island of Es Colomer, off the north coast of the Formentor Peninsula, is very interesting since this area has a markedly colder, damper climate. Further study

I

of the characteristics of this particular race could prove to be very rewarding.

A final point of note is that on Minorca, in addition to sub-species of *L. lilfordi*, there exists a group of rather larger lizards showing closer affinity to the ruin lizard, *L. sicula*, races of which occur principally throughout Italy and in the Tyrrhenian Islands. The presence of this group lends additional support to the possibility of access to the Balearics from the eastward in former times.

CHAPTER EIGHT

The mammals

THE EVIDENCE PROVIDED by fossil remains leaves little doubt that the landmass that now forms the Balearic Islands once supported a rich and varied mammalian fauna. Late in the Oligocene and again on a number of occasions during the Miocene, it seems evident that Africa was joined to the vast Eurasian continent not only by way of an easterly land bridge through what is now Ethiopia, but also by way of the Iberian Peninsula. Throughout this period, which must have lasted intermittently for some 20 million years, vast hordes of the rapidly developing Palaearctic fauna were spreading south-west throughout Europe and thence into Africa. Included in these migratory streams were many representatives of the larger carnivores of the cat and dog families, together with deer, insectivores and rodents in great variety. Towards the close of this great period, the more easterly route down across Asia Minor became too arid to permit easy passage (probably much as it is today), and more and more animals tended to drift westwards. The Balearics at that time formed part of a peninsula lying to the east of Iberia, and duly received their fair share of this migratory pressure, particularly when the land bridge into Africa was severed, preventing further advance. It seems likely, however, that they too may have been cut off from the European mainland on occasions during these eras in which the main strains of our presentday mammalian fauna were beginning to differentiate.

Be that as it may, it is undoubtedly true that at the time of their final isolation and severance from the Iberian Peninsula some 800,000 years ago, the Balearics still retained a good share of this diversifying fauna. Then, however, two evolutionary calamities occurred that must have virtually decimated the animal population of the islands. In the first place, further land movements brought about a general rise in the level of the water. Though some of the more mountainous areas appear to have escaped, it is certain that much of the rest of the landmass became submerged beneath the encroaching seas. This would have the effect of imposing severe territorial restrictions on many of the larger carnivores in particular, which would ultimately bring about their extinction.

This catastrophe was followed rather later in the Quaternary by the various periods of glaciation that lasted intermittently until as recently as about 10,000 years ago. Interspersed between the various ice ages were periods of quite warm, humid climate. On the mainland of Eurasia, it seems likely that the more mobile animals responded to these fluctuations in temperature by a general southerly movement during the cold spells, followed by northerly recolonisation migrations as the temperature began to rise again. Thus both cold temperate and warm temperate fauna were able to survive on the mainland—but such a course was, of course, impossible for the land mammals marooned on the Balearics. There is little doubt that even though the islands missed the full severity of the ice ages (the nearest area of extensive glaciation being in the region of the Pyrénées), the associated climatic variations must have dealt further blows to the already severely depleted fauna. It seems to have been round about this time that many of the larger mammals became extinct.

As is only too often the case, it seems that the responsibility for the final elimination of many of the other mammals must lie fairly and squarely at the door of man. Following the last period of glaciation, much of the Balearics supported luxurious stands of coniferous and broad-leaved forest, interspersed on the lowlands with fertile grassy plains growing on the rich alluvial soil carried down from the mountains. The extensive areas of woodland would provide the mammals with a fair amount of insulation against any further vagaries of the climate, while the grasslands must still have supported a sizeable proportion of ungulates. With the coming of man about 1,500 BC or a little earlier, much of the available grassland was given over to agriculture, while the forests were rapidly thinned out by the activities of the charcoal burners at a rather more recent date. Clearance of the land resulted in rapid denudation of the surface soil, and consequently the grazing areas needed by the herbivores steadily disappeared. Moreover, as already noted, natural factors seem to have conspired with man to prevent the regeneration of the forests. As a result, though the brown bear (*Ursus arctos*) and possibly some of the ungulates and bovines are believed to have survived the rigours of the ice ages, they certainly proved incapable of withstanding for long the dawn of civilisation in the islands. Now only the last remains of a once teeming fauna survive, and there is every likelihood that the few remaining carnivores will be doomed to extinction unless urgent steps can be taken to safeguard them.

The wild boar (*Sus scrofa*) which in any case prefers a rather higher degree of humidity than the islands can provide, has long been extinct, and the red fox (*Vulpes vulpes*), once plentiful on all the larger islands, probably finally became extinct early in the present century. Both species were much prized for the pot, making very good eating, and the skins also had considerable value. The fox further contributed to its own downfall by its predatory raids on the chicken farms: its place in this respect has been gratefully taken over jointly by the red kite (which also suffers heavily at the hands of the farmers) and the booted eagle (which so far seems to be faring rather better).

Of the other larger carnivores, only the pine marten (*Martes martes*) and the genet (*Genetta genetta*) are known with certainty to survive. Both are extremely shy animals, so that numbers are difficult to assess, but it seems likely that the pine marten is now down to the last few individuals (probably of the order of a dozen or so) though the genet may be in a rather better state.

In the Balearics, the marten is now confined to Majorca, where it continues to be the victim of perpetual, often unreasoning persecution—for its prey appears to consist in the main of various small rodents, the elimination of which should prove to be beneficial to the peasant farmers rather than otherwise. The most frequent records still, unfortunately, come from the examination of gibbets, where the remains are left to rot in company with a variety of birds of prey that have suffered a similar fate. Another cause of death (though fortunately much less frequent) has been an improvement in the road network which has brought a big increase in the speed of traffic. I have found the freshly dead remains of a marten on the particularly fast stretch between La Puebla and Pollensa, where the road runs between stretches of woodland and taller maquis extending from the foothills of Tomir. Whether the relatively few fatalities caused by traffic accidents is attributable to the agility of the marten or its general scarcity is difficult to determine, though the former is perhaps the more likely, since the rather more plentiful genet is likewise only a very occasional victim.

Though the pinewoods constitute the preferred habitat of the marten, both along the coastal sand dunes and in the higher tracts of woodland, it is difficult to find in these situations. Fortunately it also frequents the boulder-strewn mountain flanks where the trees are more thinly distributed, and suitable lairs abound in the many crevices in the limestone cliffs. Here it becomes active just before dusk, and may afford brief glimpses as it ferrets among the rocks or in the thin stands of pine. At times it will show for an instant outlined against the evening sun as it slinks over an outcrop, but the short Mediterranean twilight soon hides it from view, making such sightings a rare event for the lucky naturalist.

The genet is more strictly nocturnal than the marten, and is in consequence even more difficult to discover. This attractive animal with creamy-buff body blotched with dark chocolate, long, bushy, ringed tail, pricked ears and curiously short legs almost gives the impression of having been put together from a set of spare parts, yet for all that it can be surprisingly graceful and agile in its movements. Already of rather sparse and local distribution in suitable areas of south-west Europe, and evidently steadily decreasing in these locations, it would already appear to be well on the way to suffering the fate of most of the large European carnivores. The Majorcan population, however, does not yet appear to be in too precarious a situation, though still in urgent need of protection, as there have been quite a few sightings in recent years. Preferring the stretches of damper woodland, it occurs most frequently on the northern slopes of the mountain chain in shady, secluded areas, but it will also take to the olive groves, and has on occasion been recorded from some of the more thickly wooded lowland areas—notably around Soller and along the east coast. The pelt of this species is still highly prized by the islanders, though, fortunately, trapping is now much restricted.

The true wild cat (*Felis sylvestris*), more heavily built than the domestic cat, with characteristically short, bushy, blunt-tipped tail, may still be found in the more remote stands of woodland, and is also believed to be present on other of the larger islands of the Balearic group. In common with feral cats, it used to raid the smallholdings for chickens, in most cases meeting with the usual fate. There do not appear to be any recent records of animals being trapped, and sight records by casual observers are always rather suspect (since feral cats are quite plentiful, particularly on the higher land)—nevertheless, occasional descriptions of unusually large cats seen clearly in the light of car headlights are difficult to discount, and one that I saw myself near Pto de Pollensa carrying some fairly large prey had the characteristic build and tail shape.

The weasel (*Mustela nivalis*) is still quite plentiful in most areas of richer garigue and maquis vegetation, and also on cultivated land, where it preys principally on the smaller rodents, though apparently not averse to the occasional insect snack to supplement its diet. Throughout most of the year, weasels also occur well up in the mountains, where they are active both by day and night. During the height of summer, however, they become distinctly scarce in their usual haunts, when the droughts tend to reduce the normal activity of their prey to a minimum. At such times, it appears that they move to damper ground—the shady woodlands and more particularly the marshlands of the Albufera and Albufereta together with the few remaining water courses, where the rodents are still active, and insect life is flourishing.

Rather surprisingly, in view of the abundance of insect life almost throughout the year, the true insectivores are reduced to two or possibly three species. The endemic form of the white-toothed shrew (*Crocidura balearica*) is a rather large shrew with pale underparts and a sprinkling of shaggy hairs on its coat and tail. The closely related *C. russula* is found throughout much of Europe, and there is some doubt as to whether the Balearic form warrants more than subspecific status, though it is distinctly paler on the belly, longer in the tail, and rather duller on the underparts. It occurs fairly commonly in the vicinity of human habitation, notably around the smallholdings, and in the vicinity of the marshes, and has been recorded from both Majorca and Minorca, but not yet from Ibiza it would seem. This nevertheless indicates a probable spread, since at the beginning of the present century Thomas could give very few records despite the fact that the species is usually easy to trap. A possible reason for its success could be the steady decline of the larger carnivores, though avian predators must now take a fair toll.

The minute Etruscan shrew (*Suncus etruscus*), one of the smallest European mammals, is also believed to occur sparingly in the Balearics, but the evidence so far is rather inconclusive. One of the most fruitful sources of information about the distribution of these small mammals comes from an examination of the furry pellets cast up by birds of prey: teasing these apart often discloses the bones (particularly jaw bones and incisors) of small mammals, which in many cases can be specifically identified. Any such bones should be preserved for museum examination.

The Etruscan shrew is more characteristic of olive groves and oak woods on the European mainland, and hence is rather more likely to escape notice than some of the other smaller mammals. Its secretive nature and largely nocturnal habits do not help matters, and any records of its occurrence would thus be gratefully received.

Perhaps the most interesting of the Majorcan mammals is the vagrant hedgehog (*Aethechinus algirus*)—for whereas most of the other animals show affinity with typical Eurasian forms, this is a species of North African origin. Apparently having spread into south-west Europe during one of the interglacial warm spells (strongly suggesting the presence of a land bridge with North Africa at this period) it was one of the few species of southerly origin to survive the more recent ice ages, possibly accompanied by the shrews. Whereas its status on the European mainland is now that of an extremely local resident, being virtually confined to a few coastal areas of Catalonia and the South of France, the less extreme climate of Majorca appears to suit it well, and it occurs in quite good numbers on all the larger islands. It is noticeably paler than the common hedgehog (*Erinaceus europaeus*), which does not occur in the Balearics, having creamy-buff underparts and a spineless forehead. It is on the move virtually throughout the year, only going into intermittent hibernation during short spells in the very severest of Majorcan winters when the temperature drops below 43-4° F (6-7° C). Unfortunately it now figures very high on the list of road casualties, though this does not yet show any signs of producing any material reduction in its status.

Bats are particularly well represented in the Balearics, not only around the vicinity of the villages and resorts, but also roosting in large colonies in the multitudes of limestone caves in the cliffs and mountain slopes. Bats are, however, notoriously difficult to take in traps, and to identify: on top of this, they seem to be just about the only form of animal life that the locals have no great desire to shoot (though a number of records have come to light in this way), so it will come as no surprise to learn that detailed information as to which particular species inhabit the Balearics is still rather hard to come by. Here is

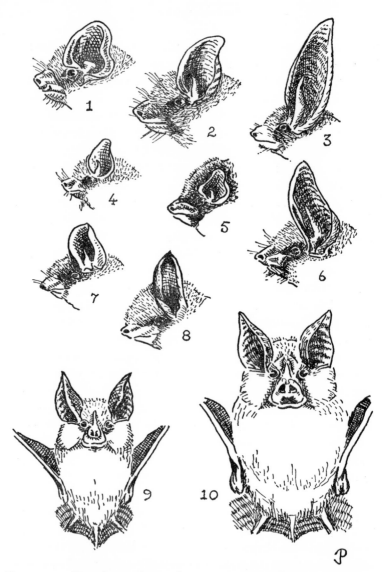

Figure 15   1 Noctule *Nyctalus noctula*; 2 Serotine *Vespertilio serotinus*; 3 Long-eared Bat *Plecotus auritus*; 4 Pipistrelle *Pipistrellus pipistrellus*; 5 Schreiber's Bat *Miniopterus schreibersii*; 6 Large Mouse-eared Bat *Myotis myotis*; 7 Natterer's Bat *Selysius nattereri*; 8 Long-fingered Bat *Leuconoë capaccinii*; 9 Lesser Horseshoe Bat *Rhinolophus hipposideros*; 10 Greater Horseshoe Bat *Rhinolophus ferrum-equinum*

another field where the casual visitor can contribute much valuable help by taking accurate drawings and measurements of any bats that he may happen to come across in the course of his holiday. Overall length, 'wingspan', 'wing chord', and shape and size of ears in relation to the head are the most valuable aids, but the animal should also be photographed if at all possible.

Many of the European bats are, of course, highly migratory, so that it is difficult to single out (other than by frequency and seasonal distribution of records) which species are resident— indeed it could well be that a number of the southern European or circum-Mediterranean species are somewhat nomadic in habit, appearing to occur more frequently at particular places in some years than in others, and moreover, not being too particular as to season, so that the whole picture is obscure and in need of clarification.

The most common and widely distributed representative of this order in the lowland areas of Majorca is the long-eared bat (*Plecotus auritus*), a species of widespread European distribution and strongly migratory tendencies. It regularly disappears into hibernation for two or three months during the depths of winter, when the temperature falls much below about 46° F (8° C), though the equally migratory and nearly as widespread pipistrelle (*Pipistrellus pipistrellus*) seems to be on the wing almost throughout the year. Two other species every bit as cosmopolitan, yet as the available records suggest for some reason less well represented in the Balearics are the serotine (*Vespertilis serotinus*) and the noctule (*Nyctalus noctula*). The latter has been taken in Majorca on a number of occasions, more typically in winter and spring, but the serotine is apparently only known for certain from Ibiza. Since both species are highly migratory, it is possible that there is a general exodus from the islands following birth of the young, which takes place in early spring. Superficially rather similar (though the noctule has warmer brown colouring, and is distinctly more slender) there is a danger of confusion, and sight records need to be treated with great caution, especially so as both species are quite often on the wing well before dusk. As with all bats, careful examination in the hand is the only way to really clinch the identification.

The large mouse-eared bat (*Myotis myotis*), one of the few that can be identified with a reasonable degree of certainty by sight alone, in view of its noticeably large size and forward-pointing pricked ears, is quite likely to attract the attention. A typically temperate species, it occurs in the vicinity of stretches of wood-land and the taller maquis vegetation of the lowlands and moun-tain slopes, but does not appear until after dark. Though most active in spring and early summer, and again in autumn, it can remain on the wing throughout all but the most severe winters. In some areas it tends to associate with the rather smaller Schrei-ber's bat (*Miniopterus schreibersii*), but in Majorca the latter is much more a species of the mountain slopes, finding in the limestone caves ideal roosting-places, and usually appears on the wing well before dusk.

Less well known, and infrequently recorded in recent years, are the highly migratory greater and lesser horseshoe bats (*Rhinolophus ferrum-equineum* and *R. hipposideros*). Being wide-spread throughout Europe, they would be expected to occur with much greater regularity, so the sparsity of records may indicate that these species are perhaps no more than occasional migrants through the Balearics. Natterer's bat (*Selysius nattereri*) tends to be more partial to a cooler climate, so being at the southern limit of its normal range, the paucity of records for this species are not by any means so surprising. As it flies much nearer the ground, and follows a rather less erratic course than most other bats, it is more easily taken—indeed it may on occa-sions blunder into mist nets set up at dusk to trap migrant birds.

Three other bats of much more localised Mediterranean distribution occur in the Balearics, these being Kuhl's and Savi's pipistrelles (*Pipistrellus kuhlii* and *P. savii*) and the long-fingered bat (*Leuconoë capaccinii*). The first two have been obtained at various seasons and as there is no reason to suppose that they are particularly migratory species, should probably be regarded as resident, but the status of the long-fingered bat is still obscure:

it is of very restricted distribution, and may be no more than a casual visitor from the mainland. As already noted, however, it is not unlikely that all three species may be somewhat nomadic.

Turning to the *Leporidae*, we find only the rabbit (*Oryctolagus cuniculus*) and the brown hare (*Lepus capensis*)—the Balearics lie well to the south of the normal range of the blue hare (*L. timidus*). During the nineteenth century, despite the presence of natural predators such as the fox, the rabbit used to be fairly plentiful: it appears, however, that the decline of predators has been more than compensated for by the use of the gun, and nowadays rabbits are quite thin on the ground, though here and there the peasants breed them—at first as pets, but later, doubtless, for the pot. The hare, though likewise rather poorly represented, is rather more generally distributed, and can be encountered at quite high elevations in the mountains. It feeds among 'soft' grassland right up to the limits of the tree zone, but the areas of *Ampelodesmus* grass prove too tough for its liking. As with the rabbit, it is much prized for the pot, but frequenting rather less accessible areas, is perhaps less severely persecuted. The Balearic form is quite distinct from its more northerly counterpart, having longer ears with more pronounced black tips, more black on the tail, and a darker, mottled back: it is to all intents and purposes a more extreme version of the Iberian form.

Rodents are well represented—in particular the garden dormouse (*Eliomys quercinus*), which, though its name suggests association with oak woods, seems to be more typical of the coniferous woodland in Majorca, though also frequenting olive groves and the orchards. The wood mouse (*Apodemus sylvaticus*) also rather belies both its scientific and common names, as it is more essentially an animal of open country and areas of scrub maquis vegetation, being every bit as much at home in the rocky parts as well as among richer herbage. The house mouse (*Mus musculus*) is polymorphic, and occurs in two main colour phases —the grey form associated with human habitations, and a browner, white-bellied form with shorter tail found more typically among low vegetation, where it comes to some degree into competition with the wood mouse. All these small rodents must form a staple item in the diet of the many predatory birds that inhabit the Balearics.

The brown rat (*Rattus norvegicus*) has now largely ousted the black rat (*R. rattus*) from the vicinity of human habitation, and has also colonised the areas of saltmarsh (particularly the Albufera, where its excessive tunnelling operations often undermine the dykes bordering the drainage canals): here it is taken for food—though the locals will not touch the rats of the villages and towns, probably due to the long association of the black rat with the spread of disease. On a couple of occasions, I have seen on the Albufera small, short-tailed 'water rats', and Henry Tegner informs me that he recently saw prints and droppings that seemed to his experienced eye to be characteristic of the water vole (*Arvicola amphibius*), but these observations have not yet been confirmed by definite evidence.

Finally, brief mention must be made of the feral goats that manage to find frugal sustenance among the coarse grasses and thin, often spiny vegetation of the high peaks. The males make a fine sight when outlined on some rocky buttress against the evening sky, huge spread of horns held proudly above strong shoulders. Periodically they are herded into corrals, where they are culled for their skins, which are much sought after, and provide the raw materials for a number of local craft industries. Many of the sheep are also allowed to roam wild in the Sierras: in colour, build and spread of horns, they are reminiscent of the mouflon (*Ovis aries*) suggesting cross-breeding with animals from the Tyrrhenian Islands, where the mouflon is indigenous.

Perhaps the biggest mystery of the Balearic fauna is the complete absence of the red squirrel (*Sciurus vulgaris*), which is also absent from others of the larger Mediterranean islands, yet is still quite widespread elsewhere in Europe. This animal is thoroughly at home in stands of coniferous woodland, and there would appear to be ample territory available. The species is, however, prone to epidemics which could perhaps run through a complete island population. Nevertheless, it is striking to note also that birds such as the jay and woodpeckers, with similar preference for extensive woodland habitat on the mainland, are also conspicuous by their absence.

Though it may not be strictly in order to include cetaceans in the content of an island's ecology, nevertheless the atmosphere of Majorca is such that thoughts of the sea are never very far away. One is tempted to while away long hours seated on the clifftops gazing out over the deep, pure blue of the Mediterranean, or down into sheltered coves where the water laps deep green over fine silver sand: and at such times it is not uncommon for one's attention to be attracted to schools of some of the smaller cetaceans passing offshore—perhaps in the wake of some pleasure boat, or even accompanying flocks of gulls or migrating terns. Occasionally too, one may be rewarded by glimpses of the characteristic features of one of the larger whales; perhaps the massive head and forward-arcing spout of the sperm whale (*Physeter macrocephalus*) which, being essentially a subtropical species, finds its way into the confines of the Mediterranean quite frequently. Or it may be the narrow, triangular, upright dorsal fin of the fast-moving killer (*Orcinus orca*) cutting shark-like through the water, or less frequently the backward-sloping fin of the smaller false killer (*Pseudorca crassidens*)—both deep-water species these, but by no means unknown from the vicinity of the Balearics.

The common dolphin (*Dolphinus delphis*) is without doubt the most abundant of the cetaceans, frequently frolicking about offshore vessels and associating with seabirds—or rather the reverse, for the birds tend to follow the cetaceans in the hope of finding an easy meal. The bottle-nosed dolphin (*Tursiops truncatus*), of more northerly cool-temperate latitudes, and the more pelagic, heavy-headed Risso's dolphin (*Grampus griseus*) are much less frequent, but enter the Mediterranean fairly regularly in small schools and have both been recorded off the islands: the pilot whale (*Globicephala melaena*) is much rarer, and usually only occurs this far south in the middle of winter.

More typically inshore species include the common rorqual (*Balaenoptera physalus*) and lesser rorqual (*B. acutorostrata*), the latter at times following ships, and on rare occasions both are known to have been beached following heavy storms in the western Mediterranean. The likelihood of such an event occurring nowadays, however, is becoming increasingly remote, as excessive persecution continues to threaten the future of the rorquals.

Other deep-sea cetaceans enter the Mediterranean apparently by accident when on migration, but they rarely spread far into the western basin, though Cuvier's whale (*Ziphius cavirostris*) has reached the Tyrrhenian Islands, and is perhaps the most likely to turn up off the Balearics. Lastly, it must be put on record that the deep brown monk seal (*Monachus monachus*), a never very common species that is steadily declining and now becoming quite rare and more restricted to the eastern basin of the Mediterranean used to breed in scattered small groups along the south-east coast of Majorca as recently as early in the present century, but has been extinct there for over thirty years. This is a species that appears to be in drastic need of conservation in its few remaining haunts if it is to survive.

CHAPTER NINE

Bird life in Majorca

In recent years, Majorca has become very popular in ornithological circles, as a holiday centre for the observation of
spring migration through the Mediterranean, and in later pages
this aspect of the island's ornithology will be treated in some
detail. But it was really the lure of the many rare and local
breeding species that are to be found within its limited confines
that first attracted the attention of bird watchers. Yet this wealth
is by no means obvious at first glance, for the gun is still an all-
too-familiar object in the countryside, and many of the resident
birds look warily upon the intruder: the ornithologist often has
to work hard for his rewards.

But this having been said, we must put the question: where
else in Europe could one go to spend a morning watching upwards of twelve species of predator, including that king of
birds, the black vulture, hunting along mountain flanks or ther-
malling ever upwards until lost to sight in the limitless blue vault
above? And then, perhaps, come down to be entertained by a
raucous colony of black-winged stilts breeding on the marshes
below, lunch at a rocky headland cooled by the salt spray
(keeping a weather eye open to catch feeding movements of
Cory's and Balearic shearwaters, accompanied by the occasional
Audouin's gull), spend a hot afternoon quartering the harsh
garigue for Thekla larks and the elusive Marmora's warbler,
and if this is not enough, stop off for a few moments on the way
back to a well-earned dinner to whet the appetite by witnessing
the evening gathering of Eleanora's falcons, swooping and playing over the salt-pans in the brief Mediterranean twilight. Where
else could all this happen in one day, and still leave room for

K 161

more? More important, where else could it happen with only a mere 50 miles (80km) recorded 'on the clock'? It is this very combination of accessibility and variety that makes a visit to Majorca such an enjoyable and rewarding experience, even though it may be for a mere two or three days.

BIRDS OF PREY

There is no doubt that it is the indescribable fascination of predator-hunting that has been responsible in the first instance for attracting many a naturalist to the Balearics. Somehow the extremely restricted mountain terrain of Majorca manages to support a truly amazing variety of raptors, the very names of which conjure up visions of wild loneliness and unscalable heights. Yet these same mountain fastnesses that are so essential to the survival of these great birds continue to be steadily eroded to satisfy the voracious appetite of the holiday industry, with its insatiable demand for more and more hotels. As roadways and construction work continues to invade the privacy of the birds of prey, it will come as no surprise to realise that some species are in a critical state bordering on extinction, and in urgent need of special conservation measures.

The rare and elusive Bonelli's eagle, for example, typically a bird of the upper limits of the forest zone, is reduced to at most three or four pairs—a status that does not appear to have changed materially over the last thirty years, when Bernis noted it as being on the verge of extinction. The main population is localised in the Valldemosa/Soller area, from where occasional birds stray to the Formentor and Arta Peninsulas. Along the higher mountain slopes of the Sierras, it is sometimes possible to see these great birds, often in pairs, swinging swiftly through the treetops with short bursts of quite fast wingbeats, or soaring out across the valleys: in fact the whole behaviour and flight action of this species is much more like that of an outsize hawk than of an eagle—a point which could cause some confusion in the early stages of identification.

A general tidying-up of the island, again in the interests of the tourist trade, has decreased the supply of carrion, bringing in its wake the virtual elimination of the Egyptian vulture. As recently as the 1930s, it still had residential status, but it is now no more than a summer visitor, usually arriving in April, in very small numbers. Rarely more than two pairs breed, and in some years none are recorded at all.

A perhaps rather less obvious case for conservation is provided by the red kites. These birds enjoyed a brief period of success in their raids on chicken farms following the decline of the mammalian predators, but they soon began to pay for their temerity, and the larger farms and estates now take a steady toll —as their gibbets give eloquent evidence. The north-west Sierras may still support some 10–12 pairs with perhaps another 2–3 pairs on the Arta Peninsula, but this probably represents about a 20 per cent decline during the last decade—which gives cause for immediate concern.

On the credit side, it is pleasing to be able to draw attention to the continuing healthy state of the resident black vulture colony. Several estimates of the population in the late 1960s gave figures of about 30–35 birds, but in a thorough survey of the Sierras undertaken in August 1966, J.-M. Thiollay quoted a total of at least 67 resident birds. Whichever estimate is the more accurate, this must surely represent one of the highest concentrations of this magnificent but distinctly local vulture in the whole of Europe. How they manage to survive remains a mystery: a sizeable part of their food supply must consist of weakly kids and lambs, but it is difficult to see how there can be sufficient of these to fulfil their demands, and the higher peaks which are their domain hold little else in the way of animal life apart from a few rodents. Munn recounts an incident of a vulture contemplating dining off a member of the local police force, who was enjoying a siesta under a bush: he awoke in some panic, and shot the bird, so this can hardly be taken as evidence that human beings form a staple dietary item.

The status of the osprey is also encouraging. During the late 1950s and early 1960s there was some indication of a widespread decline in numbers of the fish-hawk, particularly in the USA, but the Majorcan ospreys held their own, and in common with the British stock the last decade seems to have seen a slight improvement. There are 8–10 eyries along the north-west coast that are fairly regularly occupied, together with another 2 on the Arta Peninsula, and others on Cabrera and Dragonera—off the south and west coasts respectively. Birds from Cabrera often come across to feed around the Salinas de Levante. Though one pair of ospreys may have 2 or 3 eyries that they occupy in rotation, there would appear to be at least 5 or 6 pairs breeding fairly regularly on the mainland, and another 3 pairs on off-shore islands. Up to 4 or 5 birds at a time may frequent the Albufera and nearby Bay of Alcudia on fishing expeditions, and can be watched hovering over the waters of the bay before plunging seawards in a steep dive, completely submerging beneath the waves, before reappearing, and making off for the Sierras with a large fish securely clamped in their talons. One or more birds often sit for hours quite motionless on the remains of the old shooting butts in the middle of the Albufera, before suddenly dropping on to the back of some unsuspecting fishy prey.

The golden eagle has always been of uncertain status, more typically a winter visitor, but of recent years a pair have become established in the vicinity of Ternellas, at the head of the Bocquer Valley, and there is strong circumstantial evidence that they have bred successfully, since young birds in different stages of development have been seen with adults in neighbouring parts of the Sierras. A pair of short-toed eagles also appeared near Lluch in or about 1966, since when they have been reported on a number of occasions, now and then carrying snakes or lizards. Though there is as yet no more positive proof of breeding, they seem to be well established. Brief mention must also be made of a pair of common buzzards that recently summered on mountain slopes not far from Soller: previously these birds have only been known as winter visitors and occasional passage migrants.

Booted eagles are more typical of the valleys and wooded slopes than of the higher peaks, and they may often be seen hunting near the large estates, being not averse to the occasional chicken to supplement their diet. As a consequence, they tend to suffer the same fate as the red kite, frequently ending up on the gibbet. There is no sign of this affecting their status yet, however, in fact if anything they seem to be on the increase, their numbers possibly being augmented by immigrant birds that arrive very early in the year, often before February is out.

Estimates of the breeding strength during the 1967 and 1968 seasons (based on pairs holding territory) suggested the presence of some 14-19 pairs on the mainland, together with others on the offshore islands. Bernis has queried its status as a resident, but counts of up to 10 birds are just as frequent during winter. Pale phase birds outnumber the dark by about 3:1 in the resident population, and apparently (though there are relatively few data) on migration also. There is, however, the possibility that some dark birds may be mis-identified, since they are by no means as easy to diagnose as the prominent black-and-white pattern of the underparts of the pale phase.

Booted eagles when hunting have a distinct flight pattern, in which they hang almost motionless, swaying on the breeze, before half closing their wings and dropping in a steep forward glide to pounce on, and envelop their prey. By contrast, the red kite usually swoops down and picks its prey up from the ground in a continuous forward rush.

Most of the other large predators are only casual visitors to the island, or passage migrants. Black kites pass through regularly (but often at a considerable height) from about mid-March to early May, in small flocks of half a dozen at a time, and the honey buzzard has come to be recognised in the last few years as an even more plentiful migrant, appearing in flocks of up to 20-30 during late April and well into May. The majority of these flocks of large predators move north-eastwards along the north-facing flanks of the mountains. They get lift as the on-shore breezes strengthen during the day and the land warms up under the heat of the sun, but should a cold north wind get up, bringing in extensive cloud cover over the peaks, they will drop down to quite low levels, skirting the mountain slopes, and often spend some time playing around the base of the Formentor Peninsula, apparently waiting for renewed lift before resuming their journey. Though a NNE heading is the preferred orientation for migrating predator flocks, I have seen black kites moving over Ternellas at a great height, heading WNW on warm sunny days in April.

In passing, it is interesting to note that griffon vultures have been recorded on two or three occasions in the last decade—twice following a period of WNW winds over the western Mediterranean. This suggests that the birds may have drifted across from the Iberian Peninsula, after having been taken up on a thermal, yet one of these small parties later left Formentor on a NNE heading, suggesting that they were genuinely on passage.

The smaller predators are also well represented in Majorca, kestrels being particularly numerous both on the wooded mountain slopes and among the taller maquis vegetation of the lowlands. The lesser kestrel was formerly regarded as a rare spring migrant, and Munn even went so far as to question the authenticity of records prior to the 1930s, but now small numbers are recorded on passage almost every spring, and there are occasional records of birds summering. The elegant little red-footed falcon is also turning up with increasing frequency on spring passage—often in small flocks with other drifted migrants following spells of essentially easterly winds. They occur most frequently during the first week in May, in parties of up to 5 or 6. In contrast, the hobby remains surprisingly elusive, and though fairly regular on passage in spring, it is rare for more than 2 or 3 birds to show up in any one season.

Peregrines still breed rather thinly around most of the coastal cliffs, though numbers seem to have declined here as elsewhere in Europe. There is also less sign of the winter influx, that used to begin about November—in fact if anything there appears to be more birds about during the breeding season than at the turn of the year. The merlin is now very infrequently recorded, and then usually as a winter visitor.

Black vultures apart, the most interesting Majorcan predator —and certainly in terms of its European distribution, the rarest— is the Eleanora's falcon. This graceful little falcon breeds in quite large colonies around most of the coastal cliffs, but particularly in the north-east of the island: in the mid 1960s it was estimated that at least 160 pairs were in residence. The first birds arrive late in April, but breeding is delayed until rather late in the year, so that the young are in full growth when the first autumn migrants begin to move through. During late summer, packs of falcons patrol around the Formentor Peninsula, picking up tired small migrants that are struggling to make landfall. Before breeding, large flocks frequent the salt-pans of the Albufera, where they love to harry the hordes of swallows and swifts that congregate there to feed on hatching mosquitoes when the colder days of spring bring migration to a halt. At other times, the falcons cruise over the marshes, picking off dragonflies, which they catch by the wings, severing the body from them with one deft downward stroke of the bill. Towards dusk, the flocks gather again, to feed on beetles, moths and other insects that take to the air as the light fades.

Though what has been said above implies that Majorca harbours a wealth of birds of prey that can be rivalled by few other sites in Europe, this must not be taken to mean that all one has to do is to go up into the mountains on a fine spring day, and watch the birds sail by. On the contrary, it is quite possible to visit the peaks on several successive days, and see virtually no predators at all. In fact, the best conditions for raptors are by no means easy to define, and much work remains to be done on the flight habits of these birds. Eventually, however, one develops a sort of instinct for the job, out of which the following generalisations begin to emerge.

In the first place, soaring species tend to rise on early-morning thermals, and descend again in the evening as the land cools. They can rise at quite fantastic rates, often several hundred feet per minute, so that in the interval between seeing a bird come out of some dark trees (above which strong thermals can form quickly), finding a suitable stopping place, and getting out of the car, the birds may have gone up well over 1,640ft (500m), and be nearly out of range of the naked eye. As a corollary, soaring raptors are unlikely to be on the wing on dull days, though if there is a fair wind blowing some birds may be hunting, beating to and fro along the windward slopes. Downdraughts on the lee slopes, however, will be unfavourable to flight, and birds are unlikely to be seen on the sheltered flanks of the mountains under such conditions.

A 'fall' of passage migrants often stimulates predators to hunt —when food is short, they conserve energy by resting or soaring. Consequently a short trip along the coastline is often a useful prelude to a foray into the mountains. Further, if the passage movement should happen to involve any of the larger predators, it will often be found that the resident birds take to the air to escort them through their territories, and in fact following a flock of migrating raptors is at times a useful way of estimating the resident predator population of a particular area.

On one morning, when tired migrants were dropping in all along the coastline following a rather stormy night with north-east winds and some rain, we drove the little Seat 600 (sunshine roof fully open, of course, for predator-watching) some 25 miles (40km) from Alcudia to Lluch. In the course of half a dozen stops along the route, we recorded the following list of predators: an osprey, a marsh harrier and two lesser kestrels hunting over the Albufereta of Pollensa, while another osprey, talons securely clamped around a large fish, beat steadily along the shores of the bay, en route for the Sierras; a red kite scavenging on the outskirts of Pto Pollensa and a pale-phase booted eagle soaring and wheeling low over some pines behind the town; another pale booted and three kestrels over the slopes of the Bocquer Valley, while away to the north-east towards Cala San Vicente the resident pair of golden eagles circled slowly upwards into the blue, and further south, over Ternellas, a party of six black vultures hung poised around the peak; then on towards Lluch we met a cool breeze coming in off the sea, and a migrating flock of black kites swept low overhead, escorted by a pair of red kites below, and another watchful black vulture above and to seaward of them; just a mile further on, a pair of booted eagles slid fast down a valley slope on half-closed wings, while overhead a flash of white catching the sun revealed itself as a short-toed eagle drifting idly on the wind. A total of 30 predators of 10 different species, all in under 3 hours, can hardly be considered bad by any standards!

OTHER BIRDS OF THE MOUNTAINS

Dealing with other aspects of mountain ornithology once the predators have been covered is rather like eating cake without the icing, but there are a few other birds that deserve more than just a passing mention. In the first place, the Spanish raven, a rather smaller bird than those of the British race, occurs abundantly throughout the Sierras. On one occasion, a passing raptor had no less than 110 birds in the air at once over Casas Veyas, while counts of several score of these sociable but quarrelsome birds have been made on numerous occasions from elsewhere in the mountains. There are also a few records of flocks of small corvids being seen in various parts of the Sierras, that probably refer to choughs—the characteristic soaring, tumbling flight having been noticed—but sufficiently close views to permit of the determination of the exact species have not yet been obtained.

During the early part of the breeding season, the beautiful liquid notes of the blue rock thrush is quite a feature of the mountains. This species is fairly generously distributed throughout the Sierras, and is also present along the rocky headlands of the south and east coasts, but though its song is frequently heard, it is rather shy of human intruders, and has the annoying habit of continually disappearing from view behind rocks, giving only brief glimpses of its brilliant deep metallic-blue plumage. By contrast, the rather gaudy orange and blue colouring of the ('common') rock thrush strikes a discordant note. This is more a bird of passage, appearing irregularly during April and early May, though during 1967 at least three pairs remained to breed, and nesting has been suspected on other occasions.

Birds of the high-level woodland are relatively few, though both firecrest and blackcap are found regularly up to at least 2,625ft (800m), while the chaffinch reaches to the limits of the tree zone. The blue tit is a thinly distributed resident more typical of mountain woodland, whereas the rather more widespread great tit has a distinct preference for orchards, maquis and thin woods of the plains and lower slopes. Woodpigeons are quite scarce, and very shy, resorting to the oak woods of the more secluded mountain ranges, but the rock dove is quite common, breeding both in caves on bare cliff faces, and on thinly wooded valley sides, often in colonies of 10–20 pairs. Their presence is greatly appreciated by the resident peregrines, that keep their numbers well under control. It is interesting to note in passing that the rapid north-westerly spread of the collared dove since the late 1930s (resulting in birds invading Britain by 1960) bypassed Majorca completely, and records for this species from anywhere in the Balearics are still very rare.

Visitors to the Balearics who are familiar with the bird life of the magnificent cork-oak forests of Spain are likely to be surprised by the complete absence of magpie, jay, woodpeckers (though the green woodpecker has recently been recorded), treecreepers and the like—nor is this absence easy to explain. Can it be due to the prevalence of birds of prey, or has too great thinning out of the forests resulted in their extinction? Whatever is the reason, this is one of the great unsolved mysteries of Majorcan ornithology.

Crag martins are numerous in the Sierras, usually in small localised colonies, with the vicinity of Soller and Lluch, and the gorge of the Torrente de Pareis being particularly favoured. These birds are resident, and in winter flocks of up to 1,000 may congregate over the salt-pans at the Albufera on unusually mild days that encourage a premature hatch of insects. Pallid swifts breed in colonies around the coastal cliffs, but as they are often difficult to pick out from the screaming hordes of common swifts when silhouetted against the sky, their numbers are by no means easy to estimate: with practice, however, the rather more chunky outline and more lethargic wingbeat come to be useful identification guides. Small colonies of alpine swifts, usually numbering about 20–40 pairs regularly favour a number of locations, notably on the Arta Peninsula, near Puig Major, and on some of the offshore islets; they have even been known to breed in the cathedral at Palma, and look incongruously out of place as they join with the common swifts swooping low overhead.

Finally, it may occasion some surprise to find that the Majorcan wren is a much less confiding bird than its English relative. In the Balearics it is much more a bird of the mountain slopes and high garigue, but even there the rather weak song is infrequently heard. In fact both habitat and song suggest a much closer affinity with the North African wren (*Troglodytes troglodytes kabylorum*) than with the various British and European races.

BIRDS OF THE LOWLAND

Scrubland and maquis

This habitat is above all the terrain of the short-toed lark and, to a lesser extent, the tawny pipit. These are both plentiful summer visitors to the island, arriving usually early in April, though Munn has recorded both species up to a month earlier. During the breeding season, the harsh scolding alarm of the Sardinian warbler is also a feature of the maquis, bursting forth from nearly every clump of bushes, though the owner of the voice is often loth to put in an appearance. This handsome grey warbler with its jet-black head, pure white chin and throat,

and startling red eye-ring is an abundant resident in all parts of
the island. It enjoys a long breeding season, being not infrequently double, or even triple brooded. We have had adults
feeding young out of the nest well before the end of March,
while family parties containing newly fledged young have been
reported late into August. Munn even recorded a pair with a
partly completed nest in mid-October, 1927!

With the exception of the resident blackcap, few other scrub
warblers remain to breed regularly on the islands, though
numbers pass through on migration in spring. Recently, breeding has been confirmed in both spectacled and subalpine warblers, an eventuality which has been expected for some time, and
Munn regarded both garden and orphean warblers as rare
summer visitors as long ago as the 1930s. Though the garden
warbler is still rare in summer, the orphean is becoming rather
more plentiful in spring, and often stays late, giving rise to
suspicions of nesting.

There is, however, another warbler of quite common occurrence in a number of local concentrations, that has above all
others been responsible for bringing the bird-watcher to Majorca.
This is the elusive Marmora's warbler, clad in shades of grey
relieved by brilliant red legs and eye-ring. Its general habits and
long tail make it very reminiscent of our own Dartford warbler,
but it is much more retiring. Indeed at first acquaintance it can
prove to be a most annoying bird, as it can be chased round and
round its often quite sizeable territory for hours, continually
ticking away from just in front of one's feet, without offering
even the most fleeting of glimpses. In many cases, the secret is
often to sit down quietly near where it was first heard: *it* will
then often come to investigate *you*! Curiously enough, this
attractive warbler is often associated with another species of
very restricted distribution elsewhere, but quite common in
Majorcan scrubland—the Thekla lark. This is reputed to be a
species very difficult to identify in the field, on account of its
great similarity to the crested lark. I can only say that I have only
once seen a party of the latter in Majorca, and it was then pain-

fully obvious what they were, even before I saw Thekla for comparison. It may be that the Thekla of the Iberian Peninsula are markedly paler than the Balearic birds—I have not seen other than crested in Spain or southern Portugal—but the greyish under-wing and paler outer tail feathers should be diagnostic. Also, a very characteristic feature of the Majorcan birds is a peculiar, squelching alarm note, perhaps best rendered as 'ounsch', uttered when the territory is invaded early in the breeding season, a most un-lark-like sound. Both birds have rather broad, rounded wings, and the Thekla is particularly prone to undulate from bush to bush with flopping flight, vaguely recalling a miniature, dull-coloured hoopoe. Both Thekla larks and Marmora's warblers occur in a number of areas along the south coast from Cala Blava to Cabo de Salinas, and the former is also plentiful on the Arta Peninsula (even on the peaks), while the latter has additional strongholds near Pto Cristo, Pto Colom and in the south-west.

This same thin scrub vegetation also constitutes the preferred habitat of the stonechat (which also frequents the *Salicornia/Inula* scrub of the marshes), a species widely if thinly distributed in lowland garigue and on the mountain slopes up to about 1,310ft (400m). Munn has records of the wheatear breeding occasionally in the Balearics, but it is doubtful if any remain to breed in Majorca nowadays, although many pass through on migration. The whinchat appears, often in fair numbers, later in the season, and has been suspected of breeding on a few occasions.

Larger denizens of the scrubland include the red-legged partridge and the stone curlew, both of which are most plentiful in the south-east, particularly in the vicinity of S'Avall and Cabo de Salinas—in fact on some of the larger estates such as S'Avall the partridge is now reared for shooting. Finally, no mention of the scrublands of the south would be complete without referring to the few small colonies of bee-eaters that are located near the coastline between Cala Pi and Cala Santany: in 1969, half a dozen small colonies supported a total of some fifty pairs of these brilliant, multi-coloured birds.

The larks and pipits are also attracted to the richer, cultivated land, and here linnets, and more particularly goldfinches, are numerous, small flocks congregating on waste ground everywhere to feed off the multitude of thistle-heads in late spring, to the accompaniment of a constant tinkling chorus. The corn bunting is rarely found far from cultivation, and its jingling call is a regular feature of the countryside—perhaps more particularly in the south-west of the island, but the cirl bunting, though also of fairly widespread distribution, is much more retiring in habit, prefers wilder country, and is consequently rather less frequently recorded. Surprisingly, however, this is one of the few species that tends to show up rather more frequently in autumn, when occasional passage movements are believed to occur.

Woodland

This habitat is the domain of other finches, and in particular lowland pinewoods throughout the islands are characterised by the soft, melodious 'jingling keys' twittering of serins, and the chirping of crossbills. The Balearic crossbill (*Loxia curvirostra balearica*) is worth more than passing interest, as it represents a relict population living in almost complete isolation from the main lines of development of the species in the pine forests of northern Europe (though very occasionally during eruptions these northern birds may reach Iberia, and even remain to breed for a season). The main distinguishing feature of males of the Balearic race is a distinct greyish cast to the plumage, possibly more evident in the field than in the hand, and a rather differently shaped bill. It remains to be seen whether continued felling of the pinewoods will result in the eventual extermination of this race, as would appear to have been the fate of so many other woodland birds in the Balearics.

Firecrests are as widespread in the lowland woods as they are in the mountains, if rather less conspicuous in the taller trees, and the resident blackbird comes into its own in this habitat, being very much more a woodland bird, and having a more retiring nature than the familiar blackbird of British suburban gardens. Three species that figure prominently as summer visitors to areas of richer maquis and thin woodland are the nightingale, turtle dove and spotted flycatcher (arranged in order of their time of arrival, but in converse order to their relative abundance). Nightingales arrive during early days of April, and start singing immediately, filling the woods and copses with their melodious trilling song, but many of these early arrivals soon pass on: the others arrive from a week to a fortnight later, and from then throughout the summer, the spotted flycatcher becomes one of the most characteristic birds of the island.

The borders of the woods are the special domain of the woodchat shrike. This little plump-bodied predator usually arrives with the second flush of spring migrants, following the swallows, swifts and wagtails, and when a trip to the Albufera discloses an orderly line of motionless woodchats standing sentinel on the branches of trees adjoining the marsh, the bird-watcher knows that he should be on the lookout for migrants at every turn. A fair number stay to breed on the island, but as with so many of the early spring migrants, the majority are soon winging away northwards again.

BIRDS OF THE MARSHES

As well as harbouring a great variety of typical marshland birds, the Majorcan wetlands are of great ecological importance in providing one of the few sources of water available to spring migrants on their trans-Mediterranean crossing. Reference has already been made to the shortage of fresh-water on the island during late spring and summer, and of the few permanent watercourses that remain during the migration season, the majority reach the sea either via or close to the areas of salt-water marshland. Thus the landward and central areas of these marshes often contain water of a low saline content, suitable for slaking the thirst of tired migrants. (It is not always realised that moisture loss can be a cause of greater threat to passerine migrants than lack of food, during the course of a long journey.) More will be said in later pages to indicate the importance of the marshes in relation to migration through the island.

Of the breeding birds, the first two likely to attract the attention as one approaches the marsh are usually warblers—fan-tailed and Cetti's respectively. The former is a most amusing and pugnacious little bird that dances up and down like a yo-yo over the reed-tops, perpetually uttering its zipping alarm-note. I once watched a pair of these birds chasing two marauding hoopoes out of their territory—a most ridiculous sight, for the hoopoes looked about five times their size, yet there was no doubt as to who was winning as the hoopoes beat a hasty and disorderly retreat. Fan-tails abound on the marshes, often flocking there in winter, but also frequent agricultural land. Their nest, should one be lucky enough to find it, is a most beautiful structure, built almost entirely of spiders' webs, drop-shaped, with a small entrance hole only about 2cm in diameter near the top.

In direct contrast to the fan-tail, Cetti's warbler is a very secretive bird, not unlike a large, heavily built wren in silhouette, and in its habit of creeping among low foliage, cocking its rather short tail at frequent intervals. Nevertheless, the bird-watcher is not left long in doubt as to its presence, as its shrill, scolding cry explodes from beneath his feet, shattering the peace of the marshes as the bird scutters away through the undergrowth. The phrase 'peace of the marshes' is perhaps misleading here—in fact during spring and summer the marshes hum continuously to the trilling of crickets, that provides a most restful background unless one happens to be trying to pick out the churring of Savi's warbler against the incessant noise.

Other common inhabitants of the *Salicornia/Inula* scrub are the Spanish wagtails. These attractive little birds with the half-eyestripe are very early arrivals, and I have seen them feeding young out of the nest by the beginning of April, while flocks of the other races of the yellow wagtail were still coming through on passage. These birds often swarm around the marshes during April, in parties of a few score, dancing and moth-flighting in the air as they feed on the hatching insects.

The scrub also provides one of the preferred breeding grounds for colonies of little ringed and Kentish plovers, which also nest on and around the salt-pans, on some of the beaches, and even occasionally among the pines skirting the sand dunes. The Kentish plover has been a common resident in Majorca for many years, but there was some concern as to whether it would be able to withstand the steady spread of the rather more aggressive little ringed plover that commenced early in the present century. The latter began to make regular appearances in Majorca early in the 1920s, Munn recording the first nest in March 1921, and the first for Minorca two years later. Throughout the succeeding decade, he watched the rapid increase with some degree of trepidation, and on a number of occasions recorded instances of little ringed plovers ousting the more retiring Kentish plovers from former breeding sites. Fortunately his fears have proved groundless, as the main flood-tide of the advance has long passed Majorca leaving a comfortable excess of Kentish plovers in its wake. In some years, however, there seems to be a renewed surge on the part of the little ringed, particularly evident in passage flocks of a noisy, quarrelsome disposition, and the breeding stock often shows a marked degree of fluctuation from year to year.

Kentish plovers flock during winter, when parties of fifty or more frequent both the Salinas and the salt-pans of the Albufera. These break up during February, and breeding commences early in March and continues well into July, some birds being double brooded in favourable years. Little ringed plovers, on the other hand, only begin to arrive in March, and many of the early arrivals pass on: the breeding season of those that remain usually begins about ten days later than for the Kentish, which may be a factor in the continuing success of the latter. The earliest

L

dates that I have for young out of the nest are 11 April 1967 and 11 April 1968 for Kentish, and 19 April 1968 for little ringed plover.

The breeding colonies of black-winged stilts are without doubt the showpiece of the marshes. The earliest reliable breeding record seems to be that provided by v Jordans in 1913, but since then numbers have built up steadily, until during the late 1960s the Salinas de Levante held between 60 and 120 pairs, with smaller concentrations in the more remote areas of the Albufera, and odd pairs at one or two other sites. The first birds arrive at the end of March, but breeding does not usually commence for another month or so. These lovely pied birds with slender bill and almost ridiculously long crimson legs are surprisingly elegant on the ground, and not at all ungainly. When disturbed by a passing predator, they make a wonderful sight hovering and beating around the colony, yelping in agitation until it disappears from view.

The predators concerned in these forays are principally marsh harriers. Both the Salinas de Levante and the Albufera support up to 5 pairs of these large hawks, with another pair or two based on the Albufereta of Pollensa. During the mid 1960s, however, Montagu's Harriers—usually casual passage migrants —were noted to be making a longer stay on the Salinas than usual, and in the spring of 1967 2 breeding pairs were located there within 100ft (30m) of each other. One of these pairs hatched 5 young, 3 of which eventually left the nest, but their subsequent fate (and that of the other pair) remains unknown. In this year also, a male hen harrier, and possibly a pair, summered, but breeding was not recorded.

The beds of bulrushes and the drainage channels with their stands of *Phragmites* shelter a good variety of small passerine species, including the resident moustached warbler, of dark-streaked crown and pure white eyestripe. An endemic race of the reed bunting, with a rather heavy bill, occurs rather more frequently than might be supposed, on account of its retiring nature. The European form occurs regularly in winter, and is much in evidence, delighting to perch on the very tops of the reeds.

Savi's warbler arrives to breed during the first fortnight in April, and reed warblers appear about the same time, but the sedge warbler is apparently of infrequent occurrence, and the marsh warbler has yet to be recorded with certainty. The scarcity of these last two is rather surprising, and it may merely be that they have been overlooked. Certainly when one hears so much these days of sedge warblers imitating marsh warblers mimicking reed warblers, etc, etc, I for one would be reluctant to accept evidence based on call alone. Trapping on the Albufera has yielded several undoubted moustached, and there are a couple of good sight records of aquatic warblers, but the only unstreaked *Acrocephalus* warblers to be taken in April have been reed warblers without doubt. The occurrence of the aquatic warbler is interesting, since this must be about the most westerly outpost of its European range. In the last decade, it has twice been recorded in circumstances suggestive of breeding, though this has yet to be proven. Rather surprisingly Munn regarded the bird as being a rare resident on the Albufera, but there are no recent wintering records at all, and it is not impossible that he was mistaken. It is not beyond the bounds of possibility, however, that it may turn out to be of fairly regular occurrence in spring.

Early May sees the main arrival of the great reed warblers. From the time of their first arrival, the strident song, delivered conspicuously from stations atop the reeds, becomes a regular feature of the Albufera. Rather surprisingly, the song is also often heard from passage birds, sometimes quite high up in the mountains—though in this case it usually issues from the vicinity of one of the occasional water storage tanks to be found there.

Coming into the heart of the marshes, we reach the home of the purple heron, which has a distinct preference for the thicker stands of bulrushes. The Albufera supports a colony of up to about 15 pairs in most years, with another 2 or 3 pairs on the Albufereta of Pollensa, but surprisingly few are reported from the Salinas de Levante. Their arrival in late March or early April usually results in a slight overlap with the wintering grey heron, which often lingers until early May, and used to breed at one time (according to Munn, who referred to a large colony on Cabo del Pinar that was eventually exterminated by shooting). Parties of grey and more particularly purple herons also move through the islands on passage, and flocks of 20–30 of the latter planing in to the marshes to rest before resuming their north-ward flight make a fine sight. They often arrive in the early morning, and stay for a few hours before circling upwards on a rising thermal to a great height and heading away due north across the Sierras, doubtless making for the Camargue.

The little bittern occurs on the marshes fairly regularly on spring passage, but the bittern itself is distinctly scarce. They both used to breed in former years, certainly up to the 1950s, and the little bittern stays long enough to lead one to suspect that it still does so. The status of this bird is probably little different from what it used to be, but in the 1930s Munn re-garded the bittern as 'a common resident on the marshes of Majorca', so there has been a marked decrease here. In contrast, Munn regarded the little egret as something of a straggler, recording only odd single birds, pairs and very occasional small flocks at this same period, whereas now parties of twenty or more are recorded on passage in most years, and a dozen or so often remain throughout the summer. The terrain seems ade-quate, and there is little doubt that given freedom from dis-turbance these graceful snowy white egrets would eventually be added to the island's breeding list.

Of the smaller waterfowl, the little grebe breeds regularly on the Albufera, and doubtless on other waters, where it occurs in scattered pairs. During the 1960s water rails bred in fair numbers on at least three marshes, and both Baillon's and little crake have been seen and heard on the Albufera and the Salinas during the breeding season, the former in May and June and the latter from late March to early May. Records based on call alone are no longer valid, and there has been no direct evidence as yet of either species having bred—indeed their status as a whole is badly in need of clarification. Spotted crakes have been heard 'whiplashing' on a few occasions in spring, but I have no recent winter records, and Bernis seems to be rather doubtful about giving them 'resident' status.

Both coot and moorhen breed along the drainage canals, but in no great numbers. The coot is principally a winter visitor, when flocks of up to 600 can occur, but the majority have left by early April: nevertheless, sufficient remain to outnumber the moorhen on all the larger marshes in most years.

Out of the large flocks of duck that frequent the Albufera and Bay of Alcudia in winter, very few remain to nest. The Albufera probably supports upwards of twenty pairs of mallard in most years, but otherwise only shoveler (which sometimes linger into May) seem at all likely to breed. Pintail often stay late, but Majorca lies well to the south of the limits of their breeding range, though Munn suspected breeding in 1927. Garganey are regular on spring passage, sometimes in parties of 20–30, when they frequent the salt-pans often in the company of waders, but though some may remain for a week or so, all eventually move on. The red-crested pochard used to breed sparingly in the nineteenth century, but decreased steadily in numbers towards its close, and there have been no recent records to my knowledge. The rare marbled teal have been recorded on a couple of occasions in spring, but there is no reason to suppose that these were other than passage birds.

BIRDS OF COASTAL WATERS

The commonest offshore birds in the Balearics are Cory's and Balearic shearwaters, the latter a race of the Manx shearwater, with sooty-brown upperparts and variable brown mottling on the underparts and underwing. In winter the eastern Mediterranean shearwater, with dark brown upperparts and pure white underparts, also visits the western Mediterranean and is often represented in longshore passage movements, particularly in

stormy weather. There is only one recent authentic record of the
nominate race of the Manx shearwater, which is blue-black
above and pure white below, and that was for mid-May.

The shearwaters breed on many of the offshore islets, and
probably on the mainland itself, where recently occupied burrows have been found on a number of occasions, notably along
the north coast. Cabrera and nearby islets hold large colonies
from which birds travel in regular feeding movements along
both the south and east coasts, while rafts of several hundred
often forgather off the Formentor Peninsula. In Munn's day,
Cory's appeared to be rather the more plentiful but the situation may have reversed slightly since then. At any event both
species occur abundantly in offshore movements, and on
favourable days with haze at sea and a stiff onshore breeze blowing, movements well into the thousands have been recorded.

Small colonies of storm petrels breed on Cabrera and probably
elsewhere. They frequently follow ships in the Bay of Palma,
and vessels fishing from the north-east ports, and up to fifty
have been noted in a flock following a school of porpoises
playing offshore. The superstitious fishermen, according to
Munn, regard it as a sign of bad luck if the birds should alight,
as they often do, on the cork floats of the nets.

The shag is resident, probably breeding on all the main islands
of the Balearic group. In Majorca it is concentrated in a series
of small colonies along the stretches of steep rocky coastline
from the Formentor Peninsula right around to Cap de Cala
Figuera in the south-west. Cormorants, on the other hand, are
best known as winter visitors in rather irregular numbers,
though they may also turn up at other times.

Despite the numerous species of gull and tern that frequent
the coastal areas and salt marshes on passage, and may from time
to time provide the odd breeding record, there are only two
species that can in any sense be regarded as resident. These are
the quite plentiful herring gull, and the at first glance not dis-
similar but very much rarer Audouin's gull. The herring gulls
are all of the yellow-legged race (*Larus argentatus michahellis*),

and small colonies are located along the north-west coast and on several of the offshore islets, though the main breeding concentration in the Balearics may still be on Minorca. In contrast, the status of Audouin's gull is much less secure. It is believed to breed occasionally on Dragonera, Conjera and possibly Cabrera, and at least one pair was strongly suspected of nesting at an inaccessible station north-east of Soller in 1967. Though numbers fluctuate somewhat from year to year, possibly representing new influxes from elsewhere, it remains essentially a very rare resident, about which definite information as to breeding is still lacking. Small numbers can be seen fairly regularly off the south and east coasts, sometimes accompanying feeding movements of shearwaters, and concentration of up to twenty-five have been recorded at odd times in the Bay of Palma and other favoured places. They could, indeed, be more plentiful than is generally supposed, for the adult is only readily distinguishable from the herring gull at close quarters, when the rather heavy-looking, black-banded crimson bill can be distinguished. Flight identification is based on the rather greater extent of less clearly defined black on the wingtips, slightly narrower wings, and more elegant wingbeat—characters difficult to define, and requiring some experience before they can be applied with any degree of certainty. Immatures are rather easier, differing from immature phases of the herring gull by showing a greater amount of grey suffusion about the head and neck: this is particularly true of first-year birds, which look distinctly grey at the front and brown at the back.

Probably the best place to see Audouin's gulls is on the rocky islets off the south coast near Colonia de Sant Jordi, particularly during periods of onshore winds. Here they become at times quite tame, and with luck can even be lured to close range by scattering food on the shore.

WINTER VISITORS

During the winter months, from about mid-October to early

April, Majorca receives large influxes of a wide variety of birds from further north in Europe, comprising mainly thrushes, finches, waders and wildfowl. The bird life is, if anything, richer during the rainy season, no doubt due to the adequate supply of fresh water, coupled with the mild climate that allows life to flourish throughout all but the coldest days of winter.

Starlings in particular flock into the Balearics in thousands during October and November. Some pass on, but many over-winter in the islands, roosting in huge black clouds in the reed-beds of the Albufera and other marshes, and also in the pine-woods. They are often accompanied by large flocks of the wintering thrushes—of which song thrushes and redwings are the most abundant, accompanied by lesser numbers of black-birds, fieldfares and mistle thrushes. Up to about 20–30 years ago, all these birds used to be extensively trapped and shot in the Balearics and sold commonly for food in the markets. They were held in great esteem for their rich flavour, attributed, according to Munn, to having fed largely on olives during the winter months (occasionally doing considerable damage to the crop). In favourable years, they were even exported to the mainland of Europe. Though this practice has now been stopped, there is little doubt that numbers still fall victim to the voracious appetites of the islanders.

Recovery of ringed birds suggests that the majority of immi-grants originate from the Baltic area, apparently roughly paral-leling the general south-westerly orientation that brings Scandinavian birds to the British Isles in autumn. Vagaries of wind and weather obviously superimpose modifications on this simple pattern, and greatly influence both the numbers and species of birds that reach Majorca in any particular winter. It is interesting to note, for example, that sample trapping on the Albufera has shown that all three races of the chiffchaff, *Phylloscopus collybita collybita* of western and central Europe, *P. c. abietinus* of Scandi-navia, and even occasionally *P. c. tristis* of Siberia, occur in winter, though members of the latter race do not appear to be resident every winter by any means. I have, however, had all three in a net together during March. All the willow warblers that I have had, however, proved to be *P. trochilus trochilus*, although the northern form *P. t. acredula* might well have been expected to occur. The willow warbler is not nearly as plentiful on the island as the chiffchaff in winter, however, being much more in the nature of a passage migrant.

Among other small passerines to winter in the Balearics, large numbers of the pale-breasted Continental race of the robin, *Erithacus rubecula rubecula*, figure prominently, being very widespread in maquis vegetation and woodland throughout the islands. They, also, used to be much fancied for the pot (and rumour has it, still are). By contrast, the Continental dunnock, *Prunella modularis modularis*, which not infrequently accompanies it on emigration to the British Isles in autumn, is surprisingly scarce in the Balearics, being restricted to thick scrub undergrowth of the rather wilder areas. Other species that winter commonly include birds of the garigue vegetation—black redstart, white wagtail, skylark and meadow pipit—all of which will also frequent cultivated land, and are particularly fond of the verges of the marshland in winter.

Of the woodland immigrants, the goldcrest is probably the most numerous and reliable, joining and if anything outnumbering the resident firecrests. The resident population of chaffinches is also swollen by immigration in some years, and small parties of siskin and brambling are of irregular occurrence, their numbers usually being directly related to the severity of the Continental winter. Should conditions prove to be particularly harsh, two or three rare visitors are not unlikely to show up. These include the alpine accentor, which has now been recorded on some half-dozen occasions since 1957, when Bernis accepted a record by the Nicolsons as the first authentic occurrence. This, however, is a species that could well be overlooked, though such an event is less likely in the case of the rather more colourful snow finch—the solitary record of which is probably quite indicative of its true status.

Similar conditions of severe weather have no doubt been responsible for the appearance of the citril finch in Majorca. Being essentially of more sedentary nature than most of the other finches, when these birds of the mountain coniferous forests do appear on the island, they appear to stay for a year or two, and attempt to breed. Such happened in the winter of 1923-4, for example, following which Henrici recorded breeding in 1924 and 1925. More recently birds appeared early in 1965, and were recorded subsequently during 1966 and 1967 without, however, any conclusive evidence of breeding, though a party of four in the vicinity of Pto Soller in mid-May, 1967, is perhaps suggestive of successful nesting.

The wader population of Majorca in winter is interesting and quite varied, though not including such large numbers as might be expected. Lapwings, in flocks of up to 1,000 on the various marshes are the most numerous, followed by snipe, which are, of course, more widely scattered. Both usually arrive late in October, and remain until the end of March. Woodcock follow in November, and remain thinly scattered in the woods throughout the winter, where they are still extensively shot. Small trips of curlew frequent both marshes and seashore, often remaining well into April, but there has never been any evidence of intent to breed. Ringed, golden and grey plover, in that order of abundance, winter most years in small numbers, but are of somewhat erratic occurrence; rather more surprising is the complete absence of knot and sanderling during the winter months, both species being noted only very occasionally on passage.

Dunlin, redshank and little stint all winter regularly in scattered flocks of fifty or so, interspersed with a few very grey Temminck's stints. They resort to the salt-pans in company with small parties of ruff and the occasional spotted redshank. Green and wood sandpipers (the latter rather less frequently) prefer pools among the *Salicornia* scrub and the smaller drainage ditches, but the common sandpiper winters more typically along the shoreline in parties of half a dozen or so.

Wildfowl are not so well represented nowadays during the

winter months as they used to be, and the reason for this is not particularly clear. In the 1920s, according to Munn, the marshes used to 'teem with wildfowl', mainly mallard and teal, while huge rafts incorporating several hundred of wigeon, pintail, pochard and tufted duck, together with a few shoveler used to frequent the Bays of Alcudia and Pollensa during the daytime, sometimes flighting in to the marshes at dusk. Of course they were heavily persecuted by shooters, but the recent decline in shooting does not seem to have been accompanied as yet by any return to former numbers. Recent maxima have been c 1,000 teal (January 1968), only about 400 mallard (December 1969) and 400 wigeon (regularly 1965-9), and nearly 300 pintail (January 1966). Pochard are down to about 50-60 in most winters, and tufted duck have become quite rare, appearing only in odd flocks of half a dozen or so. Only the shoveler appears to be thriving, counts of over 100 now being fairly frequent, while in December 1967 no less than 500 were gathered on the Albufera.

MIGRATION THROUGH THE ISLANDS

Until recently in their ornithological history, the Balearics have not enjoyed great popularity as a centre for the observation of migration. The reason for this is doubtless connected with the massive passage of raptors, storks and the like that follow the land bridges at either end of the Mediterranean. Recognition of the Straits of Gibraltar and the Dardanelles (together with a marginally less important route through Sicily and Italy) as the most important centres for the observation of trans-Mediterranean migration, was accompanied by the opening up of the estuary of the Guadalquiver and the Coto Doñana towards the end of the nineteenth century by that great naturalist and wildfowler Abel Chapman, and various others. More recently, the recovery of many of the smaller passerines ringed in northern Europe during the breeding season tended to confirm these routes as of major importance to the southerly passage of land birds in autumn, and indeed from the shape of the northern coastline of the Mediterranean, it was quite natural to assume that southing migrant hordes would funnel down into the Iberian Peninsula, Italy and Greece. There is as yet no real reason to doubt the general truth of this conclusion, as casual observation does suggest that the bulk of autumn passage does indeed bypass the Balearics. However, there are two important exceptions to this rule which the fly-line theory does not adequately explain: these concern the wader species (for which the marshes of the Camargue, away to the NNE, provide a pre-migratory gathering ground) which occur in about equal numbers on spring and autumn passage, and the wintering flocks of starlings and thrushes that, as already indicated, visit the islands annually in considerable numbers. The appearance of these latter birds in particular is more suggestive of a departure on a broad front from the coast of southern France, than of the following of some physical fly-line.

However, during the first half of the present century, the fly-line theory of migration was (deservedly) very popular, and it was quite natural to assume that the selfsame routes across the Mediterranean would be favoured by the migrants returning in spring—indeed there was the evidence of the raptor passage across the Straits of Gibraltar and the Dardanelles, together with the hosts of migrants that make landfall in south-west Spain to lend point to the argument. In 1931, Munn wrote:

> But the main stream of migration does not pass through the islands, few species only regularly follow this route; apparently it keeps nearer the mainland of Spain, as is shown by the number of species that occur as stragglers. The direction of migration is north-east and south-west, possibly to and from the mouth of the Rhone, so that stragglers that occur here are only the outer edge of the stream, and are cutting off the corner.

Now it is well known that the larger raptors do not obtain much lift over water, and indeed the same is true of the storks and cranes, both of which are of very rare occurrence in the Balearics in spring, while the raptors (though much more plentiful than was formerly suspected) are by no means commonly observed. But recent studies of the mechanics of flight and energy loss have shown that the crossing of wide expanses of water present rather less of a hazard to small migrants than was formerly realised. The direct crossing of the Mediterranean in a longitudinal direction, even at its widest extremes, should be well within the compass of an average healthy migrant, given suitable weather conditions.

Moreau, during studies of migration in North Africa, concluded that in addition to a stream of migrants moving up the north-west coast of Africa and crossing into the Iberian Peninsula, large numbers of migrant flocks regularly make the direct crossing of the Sahara on a broad front, and other authors have supported this view by observations of migrants gathering along the North African coastline in spring. Moreau further developed the idea that these migrants headed out across the Mediterranean on a broad front, making for the south coast of Europe, as soon as suitable conditions arose. Casement has recently given supporting evidence for this contention as a result of radar studies in the Mediterranean; additionally he shows a general SW–NE trend in the tracks of migrating flocks. Whether this orientation is deliberate, or partly the result of lateral drift is not easy to determine, since the great majority of his observations were made under conditions of (prevailing) westerly wind.

At any rate, it seems clear that given a continuation of light westerly winds and clear skies, a considerable volume of passerine migration must pass over the Balearics undetected—certainly much larger than was ever suspected by Munn. Visible evidence of huge diurnal passages of swifts, swallows and martins moving north-east along the flanks of the Sierras, sometimes for days at a time, involving tens of thousands of birds (often at a considerable height) tend to support this view. It appears necessary to make the important distinction between the large volume of *unobserved* migration that must pass over the Balearics in continuing favourable weather conditions, and the small volume of resting birds that constitutes the *observed* migration in these conditions. Paradoxically, weather favourable to migration is by no means necessarily favourable to the observation of such migration. The distinction soon becomes obvious when favourable conditions *cease* to exist.

As a general rule, the main factor inhibiting migration across the Mediterranean in spring appears to be a change in wind direction to a north-easterly airt. An essentially northerly airflow not infrequently affects the north coast of Majorca in spring, probably resulting from the Mistral blowing down the Rhone valley, bring cold air down from the Alps. Much of the effect of this wind is blocked by the Sierras, but the associated drop in temperature frequently brings cloud and mist, with more occasional rain, to the north of the island. This often results in small local 'falls' of migrants, that can occur quite suddenly. North-easterly winds have a more widespread effect, since they bring a more pronounced temperature drop from the cold, high-pressure Continental air-mass, and these winds can funnel right down the length of the island, bringing heavy cloud cover and frequent rainstorms. Such conditions may become widespread in the Mediterranean for a day or so, and in addition to acting in direct opposition to the migrants heading north-east, also tend to drift many of the less common migrants of a more easterly origin westwards towards the Balearics. In consequence it is not uncommon to find that under north-easterly weather conditions, the specific composition of migratory 'falls' along the east coast of Majorca tends to differ appreciably from those occurring in the south-west of the island under predominantly westerly conditions. This latter area receives predominantly leaf and scrub warblers, together with the occasional raptors (that subsequently move north-east along the Sierras), while the east coast receives predominantly chats, together with rarer birds of an easterly origin such as bluethroats, red-throated pipit, red-footed falcon and marsh sandpiper, together with the much rarer great white heron and glossy ibis (neither of which have been recorded from any of the small marshes in the west of the island). Though these generalisations appear to be fairly well founded, they are nevertheless given with a note of caution, as it must be admitted that habitat differentiation could well produce a similar effect.

Be that as it may, the invariable result is that during succeeding days, grounded migrants tend to move north-east along the Sierras, or northwards along the east coast, until both streams eventually rendezvous either on the Albufera, or, in the case of many of the passerines, on the Formentor Peninsula. At such times, the fields and woods in the sheltered valley at Casas Veyas, halfway along the Peninsula, can prove the most productive spot on the whole island. As soon as the weather ameliorates, northward passage recommences, and diurnal departure of meadow and tree pipits, swallows, martins, hoopoes, turtle doves, bee-eaters, warblers and chats can often be noted from Cabo Formentor—often with marauding falcons seeing them on their way.

Those birds most affected by adverse conditions (and most indicative of them) are the swallows, martins and swifts. On cold, blustery days in late March and April, they congregate in many thousands over the salt-pans of the Salinas and the Albufera, to feed on hatching insects—a most spectacular sight. At times they are reduced to a state of torpidity, often dropping on to the roads, and being run over in hundreds by passing vehicles. In such extremes of distress, the marshes offer their only hope of survival—and also during the migration season offer sanctuary to numbers of migrant larks, pipits, wagtails, scrub warblers, leaf warblers, thrushes and the like. At such times, while Casas Veyas provides an accurate cross-section of the migratory stream, the marshes at Alcudia and the surrounding woodlands teem with bird life of all kinds. Including the swallows and martins, the 9sq miles (15sq km) of marshland can often support at least 10,000 birds.

Often conditions that prove inimical to passerine migration also halt the passage of marsh terns, which at this season are either heading up towards the Camargue, or moving almost due east through the Mediterranean. Strong north-easterly gales during late April or early May often cause huge flocks numbering into the thousands to seek shelter over the marshes and salt-pans, often accompanied by the odd little, Mediterranean and slender-billed gulls. At such times, rather later in the season, they take the place of the swallows and swifts, that have by then largely moved on.

Finally in this section, I include some actual instances of the occurrence of these migratory falls. The first group concerns a series of counts made in the two small fields at Casas Veyas, each of which is only some 200ft (60m) square, that lie on either side of the road to Cabo Formentor, forming a clearing in the middle of the pinewoods.

8 April 1968. 10.00 hrs Wind light variable, convectional
2 hoopoes, 5 willow warblers, 1 black redstart, 3 white wagtails, 10 meadow pipits, 4 wheatears. In the evening the wind became steadily north, with a marked drop in temperature.

9 April 1968 Cold, strong NNE wind overnight, moderating
10.00 hrs: 1 rock thrush, 5 hoopoes, 55 wheatears, 5 black-eared wheatears, 20 common redstarts, 6 whinchats, 3 tawny pipits, 2 woodchats, 1 subalpine warbler, c 10 willow warblers.

12.00 hrs: 2 rock thrushes, 2 hoopoes, 24 wheatears, 16 black-eared wheatears, c 35 bee-eaters, c 60 wagtails (mainly Spanish and blue-headed), 2 ortolans, 5 nightingales, 6 woodchats, c 20 willow/chiffs, 2 black kites overhead.

15.00 hrs: 6 hoopoes, 82 wheatears, 5 whinchats, 3 pied fly-catchers, 3 nightingales, 6 blue-headed and 3 ashy-headed wagtails.
(On towards the Formentor Peninsula in the afternoon, there were many more wheatears, redstarts and wagtails, together with 2 melodious warblers.)

10 April 1968 Wind now light-moderate SE. Sunny and considerably warmer
10.00 hrs: 7 hoopoes, 2 wheatears, 3 black-eared wheatears, 20 whinchats, 16 bee-eaters, 3 cirl buntings, 4 ortolans, 10 white-throats, 2 spectacled warblers, c 45 willow/chiffs, 14 blue-

headed and 8 ashy-headed wagtails, 6 nightingales, 35 short-toed larks, 6 tawny pipits, 4 pied flycatchers, and 2 cuckoos heard nearby. Chats and larks were leaving the vicinity of Cabo Formentor regularly in small parties, wagtails, and swallows and martins were swarming on the marshes, and chats and short-toed larks were dropping in in hundreds along the east coast (at Pto Colom they were coasting north continually throughout the day).

Now, for comparison, a brief look at what the Albufera and Casas Veyas may have to offer under rather different conditions, when the main influence holding up migration was a strong north-westerly wind that could not really be felt down on the plain due to the shelter of the Sierras, though the evidence was there to see in the trails of cloud forming rapidly over Puig Major in the distance.

5 April 1971 Following cold NNW wind overnight, which still continues
Albufera: c 8,000 swallows and martins, c 3,000 common swifts, c 40 alpine swifts, 2 red-rumped swallows, 8 pratincoles, 5 greenshank, 65 ruff, 15 green sandpipers, 24 little stints, many little ringed and Kentish plover, 5 marsh harriers (probably resident, but this many are only in evidence when a 'fall' is on), c 60 willow/chiffs, c 30 Spanish wagtails, 5 nightingales, 4 cuckoos, 3 wrynecks, 1 orphean warbler.

6 April 1971 Wind shifted slightly to NNE overnight, and dropped somewhat
Albufera: swallows, swifts, etc, down to about 1,000, 20 short-toed larks, 2 black-eared wheatears, 4 bluethroats, 10 nightingales, 2 melodious warblers, 80 Spanish wagtails, 10 blue-headed wagtails, 10 tawny pipits along the verge of the roadway; waders were not investigated.

Bocquer Valley: 3 orphean warblers, 2 olivaceous warblers, many parties of willow/chiffs, 4 wrynecks, 2 golden orioles, several nightingales, c 4 cuckoos.

M

10 April 1971 After a few days of practically calm, sunny weather, strong W wind
Bocquer Valley: 3 golden orioles, few pied flycatchers, several willow/chiffs, 2–3 subalpine warblers, a few Bonelli's and odd wood warblers.

Casas Veyas: 3 red-throated pipits, 1 tree pipit, 4 ortolans, 8 pied flycatchers, 1 spectacled warbler, 2 subalpine warblers, 12 nightingales, 1 golden oriole, c 50 willow/chiffs, 5 Bonelli's warblers, 4 wood warblers, 6 hoopoes, 4 starlings, 2 black kites heading NNE.

11 April 1971 Cold WNW wind blowing most of the day. Clouding over in the afternoon
Pollensa/Lluch: parties of 3 red kites, and 3 and 4 black kites heading NE. Cuckoos and golden orioles heard. Raptors put up 6 booted eagles and an immature Bonelli's eagle, as they passed.

Formentor: 3 griffon vultures heading NNE, 2 booted eagles, 1 white-rumped swift clearly seen by several observers—the first for Majorca.
Otherwise little signs of migration. Note the preponderance of warblers, and marked lack of chats in this movement—also the greater prevalence of predators with the west winds (other parties of red and black kites, and 3 honey buzzards went through during 7–9 April).

The numbers involved in these 'falls' are not startling, and would certainly be put to shame by the Coto Doñana, for example, but it must be borne in mind that they do refer to very restricted areas, and further, such is the attraction of Majorca, that one is continually meeting someone who has just seen something somewhere else—so that rather than slog across miles of marsh or acres of garigue, one is able to flip happily from site to site in the car, and see everything that is going on almost every day. Though the island might not provide the bulk, it certainly produces the cream of European migrants!

CHAPTER TEN

In conclusion

IN CONCLUSION, IT is not really feasible to list addresses of organisations likely to assist the visiting naturalist in Majorca, because apart from the local natural history society which is difficult to contact, they do not exist. Nor is there much point in singling out routes of special interest, when the whole of the island (apart from detailed explorations) can be covered in about three days at most. There are, however, one or two comments that can be made from experience.

First of all, the desirability of choosing the north-east of the island as a holiday venue must again be underlined. Most of the ornithological, botanical and entomological 'hot-spots' will then be within easy reach: from here, the Arta and Formentor Peninsulas are half-day car trips, while the Soller/Valldemosa area and the Salinas de Levante comfortably occupy a full day each. Moreover, other naturalists of all persuasions and nationalities seek out this area, and you will be able to profit from their discoveries, particularly when migrants are moving through the island. Wherever you go, carry the appropriate *Field Guides* with you: reference to illustrations and Latin nomenclature can soon resolve otherwise insurmountable language difficulties.

A word now specifically directed to the gentlemen. On trips to the Salinas de Levante, either bypass Manacor, or else go through the main street so fast that your wife has no time to see the numerous signs pointing to the pearl factory, or you will emerge a sadder and wiser man! Similarly, if you have to pass through Inca, do so on your way back from a trip—all side roads seem to lead to *bodegas* (wine-cellars), and you will be in no condition to negotiate mountain roads afterwards. (A mere couple of glasses of wine can have drastic effects if followed by a rapid car climb of about 3,280ft (1,000m).)

Finally, it seems at times as if naturalist-hunting is a national sport of the local police, who tend to slap parking tickets left, right and centre. One school of thought says 'only pay the fines if you are sure you will be returning'. . . and of course, you will!

Appendix

THIS CHECK LIST FOLLOWS the modified Peters' order, as used in the revised edition of the *Field Guide to the Birds of Britain and Europe*—the recommended popular guide to identification. It is based on the checklist produced by Bernis in 1949, whose initials appear opposite species for which there have been no further traceable records since that date. Otherwise the interpretation of the status of each species is my own responsibility, though reference is made to the status as attributed by Bernis in cases where there is a marked difference of opinion. For modern references to rarities, new breeding records, or cases open to doubt, the initials of the authority are given. I would be grateful to receive any new records or further information, and I can be contacted for this purpose via the publishers.

RED-THROATED DIVER   *Gavia stellata*
Rare winter visitor (B)

BLACK-THROATED DIVER   *G. arctica*
Rare winter visitor (B)

GREAT NORTHERN DIVER   *G. immer*
Rare in winter, but may be more frequent than records suggest

LITTLE GREBE   *Podiceps ruficollis*
Scarce resident: breeding recorded on the Albufera and elsewhere

BLACK-NECKED GREBE   *P. nigricollis*
Occasional in winter, and possibly on spring passage

RED-NECKED GREBE   *P. grisegena*
Very rare in winter (B)

GREAT CRESTED GREBE   *P. cristatus*
Scarce in winter and on passage. Suspicions of breeding (M) probably unfounded

CORY'S SHEARWATER   *Calonectris diomedea*
Abundant resident

MANX SHEARWATER   *Procellaria puffinus*
Occasional visitor, late spring and autumn

BALEARIC SHEARWATER *P. p. mauretanicus*
Abundant resident

EASTERN MEDITERRANEAN SHEARWATER *P. p. yelkouan*
Regular winter visitor, and on passage, in good numbers.

STORM PETREL *Hydrobates pelagicus*
Resident in rather small numbers

LEACH'S PETREL *Oceanodroma leucorrhoa*
Rare in summer (B)

GANNET *Sula bassana*
Occasional offshore in winter and spring

CORMORANT *Phalacrocorax carbo*
Winter visitor and passage migrant in small numbers

SHAG *P. aristotelis*
Resident in moderate numbers

BITTERN *Botaurus stellaris*
Uncommon visitor, mainly spring. Has bred (B) and may still do so

LITTLE BITTERN *Ixobrychus minutus*
Occasional in spring. Has bred (B) and may still do so, since it has recently been
seen as late as June/July

NIGHT HERON *Nycticorax nycticorax*
Irregular on passage, mainly spring, sometimes staying late. There is a winter
record (M)

SQUACCO HERON *Ardeola ralloides*
Infrequent on spring passage, mainly in immature plumage

CATTLE EGRET *Bubulcus ibis*
Rare in winter and spring (B)

GREAT WHITE HERON *Egretta alba*
Rare and irregular in winter (JSA) and on spring passage (THE, DP et al).
Once in autumn (Or)

LITTLE EGRET *E. garzetta*
Passage migrant, often in fair numbers. Regularly stays late, and occasionally
summers. May have bred (B)

GREY HERON *Ardea cinerea*
Winter visitor, and on passage often well into May. Used to breed (M)

PURPLE HERON   *A. purpurea*
Summer resident and passage migrant

WHITE STORK   *Ciconia ciconia*
Rare vagrant, chiefly in spring

BLACK STORK   *C. niger*
Very rare vagrant in spring; 1 over the Albufera, 3/5/1968 (BL et al)

SPOONBILL   *Platalea leucorodia*
Barceló recorded rare autumn visits, in nineteenth century, but no more recent records (M)

GLOSSY IBIS   *Plegadis falcinellus*
Rare vagrant, spring and very occasionally in summer. Recorded on the Albufera 10/4/1955 (JDP) and 2–5/5/1969 (JRM)

GREATER FLAMINGO   *Phoenicopterus ruber*
Irregular on passage and in winter, sometimes in small flocks. In the 1920s, used to summer on the Salinas

GREY LAG GOOSE   *Anser anser*
Very occasional in severe winters; 22 over the Albufera in January 1966 (LL, BB)

WHITE-FRONTED GOOSE   *A. albifrons*
1 on marshes near Alcudia, 19/9/1921 (M)

BEAN GOOSE   *A. fabalis*
Very rare winter visitor (B); 1 over Sa Porassa in January 1966 (LL, BB)

WHOOPER SWAN   *Cygnus cygnus*
Very rare in winter. A juvenile at the Albufera, January 1964 (LL, BB)

SHELDUCK   *Tadorna tadorna*
Very rare winter visitor; 1 near Alcudia in February 1924 (M)

MALLARD   *Anas platyrhynchos*
Resident, and abundant winter visitor

TEAL   *A. crecca*
Abundant winter visitor

BLUE-WINGED TEAL   *A. discors*
A pair on the Albufera 3–5/5/1969 (JRM *et al*)—full details supplied

GADWALL   *A. strepera*
Rare winter visitor. A flock of c 10 on the Albufera, January 1965 (LL, BB). There are old nineteenth-century records (B), of doubtful authenticity

WIGEON   *A. penelope*
Abundant winter visitor

PINTAIL   *A. acuta*
Very common in winter

GARGANEY   *A. querquedula*
Passage migrant in spring, at times quite common

SHOVELER   *A. clypeata*
Common winter visitor, and on passage, often staying late in spring.

MARBLED TEAL   *A. angustirostris*
Rare on spring passage; 8 on the Albufera, 10/4/1965 (JDP); 1 there on 12/5/1967 (MK, JS) and 1 at Salinas de Levante, 7/5/1971 (Or)

RED-CRESTED POCHARD   *Netta rufina*
Rare visitor, which apparently occasionally breeds (B)

POCHARD   *Aythya ferina*
Winter visitor, apparently decreasing somewhat in numbers

TUFTED DUCK   *A. fuligula*
Winter visitor, appears to be decreasing and often quite scarce

FERRUGINOUS DUCK   *A. nyroca*
Winter visitor (B)

SCAUP   *A. marila*
Rare winter visitor (B); 1 near Alcudia, 4/11/1924 (M)

COMMON SCOTER   *Melanitta nigra*
Very rare winter visitor. Party of 4 in Pto Alcudia, 4/12/1928 (M)

SMEW   *Mergus albellus*
Rare winter visitor (B). A 'redhead' near Pto Alcudia, 24/12/1929 (M)

RED-BREASTED MERGANSER   *M. serrator*
Occasional winter visitor

GOOSANDER   *M. merganser*
Scarce winter visitor

OSPREY   *Pandion haliaetus*
Resident in fair numbers

HONEY BUZZARD   *Pernis apivorus*
Regular on spring passage most years, occasional in autumn

RED KITE   *Milvus milvus*
Resident in fair numbers, though apparently decreasing, also occasional on passage

BLACK KITE   *M. nigrans*
Fairly regular on spring passage; occasional in autumn

GOSHAWK   *Accipiter gentilis*
1 near Formentor, 6/4/1965 (JDP); 1 near Soller, June 1966 (RG), and another, 6/10/1968 (JDM). Probably vagrants

SPARROWHAWK   *A. nisus*
Very infrequent on passage and in winter

ROUGH-LEGGED BUZZARD   *Buteo lagopus*
1 over Formentor, 7/4/1965 (JDP). Full details

BUZZARD   *B. buteo*
Occasional on spring passage, and has summered near Soller. B regarded it as a scarce migrant and winter visitor

BOOTED EAGLE   *Hieraaetus pennatus*
Fairly common resident and passage migrant

BONELLI'S EAGLE   *H. fasciatus*
Rare resident

(IMPERIAL EAGLE   *Aquila heliaca*
At least 1, probably 2 *Aquila* sp showing pale shoulder flash near Puig Major, 12/4/1966 (JDP). M had 2 records, but B regarded it as extinct in Majorca))

GOLDEN EAGLE   *A. chrysaetos*
Rare resident and winter visitor

(WHITE-TAILED EAGLE   *Haliaaetus albicilla*
2 very high over the Albufereta, 2/5/1967 (MK, JS). Old records, including breeding on Dragonera, discounted by B)

SHORT-TOED EAGLE   *Circaetus gallicus*
Rare resident, since 1966 (JDP et al), though breeding not yet proven. (Recently immatures have been seen)

HEN HARRIER   *Circus cyaneus*
Occasional in winter, spring and summer. May have bred

PALLID HARRIER   *C. macrourus*
Rare vagrant (B)

MONTAGU'S HARRIER   *C. pygargus*
Occasional spring migrant and summer visitor. Bred at Salinas de Levante in 1967 (RB, RJP)

MARSH HARRIER   *C. aeruginosus*
Resident, breeding on the larger marshes

EGYPTIAN VULTURE   *Neophron percnopterus*
Summer visitor, and possibly passage migrant. Used to winter, and may still do so occasionally

BLACK VULTURE   *Aegypius monachus*
Resident in quite good numbers

GRIFFON VULTURE   *Gyps fulvus*
Casual visitor, usually in spring. Becoming more frequent

LANNER FALCON   *Falco biarmicus*
A pair at Cap Cala Figuera, 5/4/1966 (CED, JDP)

PEREGRINE   *F. peregrinus*
Fairly plentiful resident: not perhaps so common as a winter visitor as it used to be

HOBBY   *F. subbuteo*
Scarce on passage, mainly in spring

ELEANORA'S FALCON   *F. eleonorae*
Common summer resident

MERLIN   *F. columbarius*
Scarce winter visitor and passage migrant

RED-FOOTED FALCON   *F. vespertinus*
Fairly regular in small numbers on spring passages: occasional in autumn

LESSER KESTREL   *F. naumanni*
Several records since 1966, mostly of small numbers on spring passage, but summered in 1967 and in 1971. B regarded earlier records as doubtful

KESTREL   *F. tinnunculus*
Common resident

RED-LEGGED PARTRIDGE   *Alectoris rufa*
Common resident, preserved for shooting

PHEASANT   *Phasianus colchicus*
Bred at S'Avall in 1967, doubtless introduced

CRANE   *Grus grus*
1 over Bocquer Valley, 6/10/1971, and 6 at Salinas de Levante the following day, following strong northerly winds (Or)

WATER RAIL   *Rallus aquaticus*
Resident in fair numbers: numerous breeding records

SPOTTED CRAKE   *Porzana porzana*
Recorded both spring and autumn, possibly resident

LITTLE CRAKE   *P. parva*
Sight records: 1 in the Albufera, 28/3/1967 (JDP), and 1 on 7/5/1968 (BL et al)

BAILLON'S CRAKE   *P. pusilla*
Sight records: 1 on Salinas, 13/6/1967 (SH), and 1 found dead on or about 23/4/1969 (HS)

CORNCRAKE   *Crex crex*
Rare (B)

MOORHEN   *Gallinula chloropus*
Resident in small numbers. Breeding records

COOT   *Fulica atra*
Resident in small numbers, more plentiful in winter. Breeding records

LITTLE BUSTARD   *Otis tetrax*
Rare visitor (B)

OYSTERCATCHER   *Haematopus ostralegus*
Scarce on passage, mainly in spring

RINGED PLOVER   *Charadrius hiaticula*
Passage migrant and winter visitor. May have bred(M)

LITTLE RINGED PLOVER   *C. dubius*
Passage migrant and summer resident

KENTISH PLOVER   *C. alexandrinus*
Resident and passage migrant

GOLDEN PLOVER   *Pluvialis apricaria*
Occasional winter visitor: scarce on passage

GREY PLOVER   *P. squatarola*
Occasional passage migrant and winter visitor

LAPWING   *Vanellus vanellus*
Abundant winter visitor

TURNSTONE   *Arenaria interpres*
Rare in late spring and very occasionally winter

LITTLE STINT   *Calidris minuta*
Common on passage and in winter. May summer

TEMMINCK'S STINT   *C. temminckii*
Fairly regular on passage and in winter, in very small numbers. Uncommon in summer

DUNLIN   *C. alpina*
Common winter visitor and passage migrant

CURLEW SANDPIPER   *C. ferruginea*
Fairly common on passage. Occasionally summers

KNOT   *C. canutus*
Rare on passage, spring and autumn

SANDERLING   *C. alba*
Scarce on passage, principally in spring

RUFF   *Philomachus pugnax*
Plentiful on passage; rather fewer in winter

SPOTTED REDSHANK   *Tringa erythropus*
Regular on passage; winters in small numbers

REDSHANK   *T. totanus*
A few are resident: more plentiful on passage and in winter

MARSH SANDPIPER   *T. stagnatilis*
Since 1 at Salinas, 29/3/1967 (CED, JDP), has proved to be fairly regular on spring passage following periods of easterly winds

COMMON SANDPIPER   *T. hypoleuca*
Regular on passage and in winter: used to breed up to the 1920s, but no recent records

BROAD-BILLED SANDPIPER   *Limicola falcinellus*
1 seen and photographed at the Albufera, 5/10/1970 (Or)

BLACK-TAILED GODWIT   *Limosa limosa*
Infrequent on passage, principally spring

BAR-TAILED GODWIT   *L. lapponica*
Scarce on passage, spring and autumn

CURLEW   *Numenius arquatus*
Scarce on passage. Small numbers winter

WHIMBREL   *N. phaeopus*
Scarce, usually in late spring

SLENDER-BILLED CURLEW   *N. tenuirostris*
Rare visitor (B): breeding records unreliable (M)

WOODCOCK   *Scolopax rusticola*
Widespread in winter

SNIPE   *Gallinago gallinago*
Common in winter

JACK SNIPE   *Lymnocriptes minimus*
Few recent records: used to be not uncommon in winter (B)

BLACK-WINGED STILT   *Himantopus himantopus*
Common summer resident, and small numbers on passage

AVOCET   *Recurvirostra avosetta*
Regular on passage, particularly in spring

BLACK-WINGED PRATINCOLE   *Glareola nordmanni*
1 at the Salinas, 14/4/1966 (JDP)

PRATINCOLE   *G. pratincola*
Erratic on passage, mainly in spring. Suspected of having bred

STONE CURLEW   *Burhinus oedicnemus*
Resident in fair numbers. Also on passage (M)

GREAT SKUA   *Stercorarius skua*
Rare migrant; 1 near Cabrera, 7/5/1965 (LL, BB), and 1 off Cala Ratjada,
11/5/1968 (DIMW)

ARCTIC SKUA   *S. parasiticus*
Rare migrant; 1 off Cala Ratjada, 10/5/1968 (DIMW)

MEDITERRANEAN GULL   *Larus melanocephalus*
Irregular on passage, usually spring

LITTLE GULL   *L. minutus*
Not uncommon on passage and in winter. Erratic

BLACK-HEADED GULL   *L. ridibundus*
Common in winter and on passage

SLENDER-BILLED GULL   *L. genei*
Irregular on spring passage, and occasional in winter. May have bred (J)

LESSER BLACK-BACKED GULL *L. fuscus*
Irregular visitor (all seasons)

HERRING GULL *L. argentatus*
Quite common resident

GREAT BLACK-BACKED GULL *L. marinus*
Rare visitor: up to 3 off Cala Ratjada 8–11/5/1968 (DIMW)

COMMON GULL *L. canus*
Occasional in autumn and winter

AUDOUIN'S GULL *L. audouini*
Seen at all seasons—believed to breed

KITTIWAKE *Rissa tridactyla*
An old record, not accepted by B. More recently, a first winter bird off S'Oberta, 4/1/1965 (LL, BB)

BLACK TERN *Chlidonias niger*
Regular on passage, sometimes in huge flocks in spring during severe weather. Suspected of breeding (B)

WHITE-WINGED BLACK TERN *C. leucopterus*
Small numbers regular on passage, particularly in spring

WHISKERED TERN *C. hybrida*
Small numbers on passage: occasionally summers, and may have bred (B)

GULL-BILLED TERN *Gelochelidon nilotica*
Occasional on passage

CASPIAN TERN *Hydroprogne caspia*
Rare visitor (B)

SANDWICH TERN *Sterna sandvicensis*
Occasional on passage: also 1 off Cala Mayor in January 1964 (LL, BB)

COMMON TERN *S. hirundo*
Very occasional on passage, usually spring

LITTLE TERN *S. albifrons*
Fairly regular on spring passage, in small numbers

RAZORBILL *Alca torda*
Scarce winter visitor (B)

PUFFIN *Fratercula arctica*
B gives this species as rather common in winter, but there seem to be very few nowadays

WOOD PIGEON *Columba palumbus*
Resident in small numbers, mainly in mountain woodland

STOCK DOVE *C. oenas*
Scarce; status uncertain, probably mainly on passage

ROCK DOVE *C. livia*
Resident in quite good numbers, mountains and sea cliffs

COLLARED DOVE *Streptopelia decaocto*
1 at Cala Guya, Arta, 10/5/1968 (DIMW) and 1 at Pto Pollensa, 28/9/1971
(Or)

TURTLE DOVE *S. turtur*
Common summer resident and passage migrant

CUCKOO *Cuculus canorus*
Summer resident, but more plentiful on passage

GREAT SPOTTED CUCKOO *Clamator glandarius*
Erratic, rare migrant (B)

BARN OWL *Tyto alba*
Resident, population unknown

LONG-EARED OWL *Asio otus*
Possibly rare or irregular winter visitor; 1 in Arta mountains, 2/10/1970 (Or)

SHORT-EARED OWL *A. flammeus*
Possibly more frequent than *A. otus* (B)

SCOPS OWL *Otus scops*
Summer visitor. According to B some may winter

LITTLE OWL *Athene noctua*
Rare, erratic, may occasionally breed (B)

TAWNY OWL *Strix aluco*
May breed, or have bred (B). Noted very occasionally in spring, summer and
autumn

NIGHTJAR *Caprimulgus europaeus*
On passage, occasional; may summer

RED-NECKED NIGHTJAR *C. ruficollis*
B has doubtful old records: more recently 1 in Ternellas mountains, 12/4/1968
(WG et al)

PALLID SWIFT *Apus pallidus*
Summer resident and passage migrant in good numbers

SWIFT   *A. apus*
Abundant summer resident and passage migrant

WHITE-RUMPED SWIFT   *A. caffer*
A very tired bird at Formentor, 11/4/1971 (RD, PD) following strong WNW winds

ALPINE SWIFT   *A. melba*
Small breeding colonies. Regular on passage

KINGFISHER   *Aledo atthis*
Regular winter visitor in small numbers

BEE-EATER   *Merops apiaster*
A few small breeding colonies. Plentiful on passage

ROLLER   *Coracias garrulus*
Occasional on passage, mainly in spring

HOOPOE   *Upupa epops*
Common resident and passage migrant

WRYNECK   *Jynx torquilla*
Frequent on passage, and occasional in winter. May have bred (B)

GREEN WOODPECKER   *Picus viridis*
Heard and seen near the Albufera, 11–13/4/1968 (THE, JDP et al)

SHORT-TOED LARK   *Calandrella cinerea*
Abundant summer visitor and passage migrant

LESSER SHORT-TOED LARK   *C. rufescens*
B gives one certain record (M, 1969), also 2–3 with *C. cinerea*, 12/4/1965 and 2 on 14/4/1966 near Cabo de Salinas (JDP)

CALANDRA LARK   *Melanocorypha calandra*
1 (doubtful, B) at Alcudia, April 1957, 1 near Manacor, 26/12/1967 (JSA), and 2 first-year birds near Alcudia on 6/4/1968 (JDP)

CRESTED LARK   *Galerida cristata*
6 with *G. theklae* and *Alauda arvensis* near Lluchmayor on 12/4/1965 (JDP) during passage of larks

THEKLA LARK   *G. theklae*
Resident, locally fairly common

WOODLARK   *Lullula arborea*
Occasional on passage and in winter

SKYLARK   *Alauda arvensis*
Common in winter and on passage

SAND MARTIN   *Riparia riparia*
Abundant on passage. A few small breeding colonies

CRAG MARTIN   *Hirundo rupestris*
Locally common resident in mountains: flocks to the marshes in winter.

SWALLOW   *H. rustica*
Abundant summer resident and passage migrant

RED-RUMPED SWALLOW   *H. daurica*
Rare straggler on spring passage, with other *hirundines*

HOUSE MARTIN   *Delichon urbica*
Common summer resident and passage migrant

RICHARD'S PIPIT   *Anthus novaeseelandiae*
5 on the beach at Alcudia, 20/3/1957 (HNS), and 2 near Cabo Blanco, 22/12/ 1969 (JDP)

TAWNY PIPIT   *A. campestris*
Common summer resident and passage migrant

TREE PIPIT   *A. trivialis*
Fairly regular on passage in small numbers

MEADOW PIPIT   *A. pratensis*
Common winter visitor and passage migrant

RED-THROATED PIPIT   *A. cervinus*
Irregular on passage, mainly in spring, parties of up to 12 being recorded in recent years

WATER PIPIT   *A. spinoletta*
Occasional in winter and on spring passage

BLUE-HEADED WAGTAIL   *Motacilla flava*
The Spanish (*M. f. iberiae*) and ashy-headed (*M. f. cinereocapilla*) races breed: the blue-headed (*M. f. flava*), yellow (*M. f. flavissima*) and grey-headed (*M. f. thunbergi*) races occur in that order of abundance on passage, and the black-headed (*M. f. feldegg*) has been recorded at the Albufera, 14-16/4/1968 (JDP, DGB, WJW), and near Cala San Vicente, 25/4/1971 (Or)

WHITE WAGTAIL   *Motacilla alba alba*
Common in winter; often associates with the Black Redstart on passage

PIED WAGTAIL   *M. alba yarrellii*
Very occasional visitor, mainly in spring

N

GREY WAGTAIL *M. cinerea*
Winter visitor in rather small numbers

RED-BACKED SHRIKE *Lanius collurio*
A female at the Albufereta, 4/5/1967 (MK, JS), and 1 in Bocquer Valley, 28/9/1971 (Or)

WOODCHAT SHRIKE *L. senator*
Common summer visitor and passage migrant. Has wintered (M)

LESSER GREY SHRIKE *L. minor*
Rare summer visitors: may have bred (RG)

GREAT GREY SHRIKE *L. excubitor*
Rare, erratic visitor (B); 1 in Bocquer Valley, 5/10/1970 (Or)

WREN *Troglodytes troglodytes*
Rather scarce and retiring resident, mainly in the mountains

ALPINE ACCENTOR *Prunella collaris*
One acceptable record (B). More recently, 2 near Fornalutx, January 1964, 3 near Puig Major, January 1966 (LL, BB), and others suspected

DUNNOCK *P. modularis*
Rather thinly distributed winter visitor

CETTI'S WARBLER *Cettia cetti*
Locally common resident

SAVI'S WARBLER *Locustella luscinioides*
Regular summer resident, sometimes quite common in the marshes

GRASSHOPPER WARBLER *L. naevia*
Occasional on passage, late spring

MOUSTACHED WARBLER *Lusciniola melanopogon*
Common resident on the marshes

AQUATIC WARBLER *Acrocephalus paludicola*
Occasional on passage and in summer. One with nesting material and food in the Albufera, 3/5/1968 (BL)

SEDGE WARBLER *A. schoenobaenus*
Rather scarce on passage

REED WARBLER *A. scirpaceus*
Fairly common summer resident—also 3 birds singing in the Albufera, January 1964 (LL, BB)

GREAT REED WARBLER   *A. arundinaceus*
Summer resident in fair numbers, and passage migrant

ICTERINE WARBLER   *Hippolais icterina*
Occasional on spring passage

MELODIOUS WARBLER   *H. polyglotta*
Fairly regular on passage in small numbers

OLIVACEOUS WARBLER   *H. pallida*
Fairly regular on spring passage, in small numbers: also at El Arenal and San Telmo in July 1967 (RPC)

ORPHEAN WARBLER   *Sylvia hortensis*
Occasionally appears in fair numbers on spring passage, and sometimes stays late. Breeding recorded (M) but queried (B)

GARDEN WARBLER   *S. borin*
Occasional on passage and in summer

BLACKCAP   *S. atricapilla*
Resident in fair numbers, and passage migrant

WHITETHROAT   *S. communis*
Regular on passage, possibly more frequent in autumn, and sometimes stays late in spring.

LESSER WHITETHROAT   *S. curruca*
Rather scarce on passage, more frequently in autumn

SARDINIAN WARBLER   *S. melanocephala*
Very common resident

SUBALPINE WARBLER   *S. cantillans*
Regular on passage. Breeding strongly suspected in 1967, and proved near Sa. Canova in May 1971 (JDP)

SPECTACLED WARBLER   *S. conspicillata*
Fairly regular on passage in small numbers: breeding confirmed at Casas Veyas, and Pto Colom in May 1971 (JDP)

DARTFORD WARBLER   *S. undulata*
Very occasional in winter and early spring

MARMORA'S WARBLER   *S. sarda*
Locally rather common resident

WILLOW WARBLER   *Phylloscopus trochilus*
Common on passage: variable in winter

CHIFFCHAFF   *P. collybita*
Common in winter and on passage. Wintering flocks include *P. c. collybita* and *P. c. abietinus*

BONELLI'S WARBLER   *P. bonelli*
Regular on passage in small numbers

WOOD WARBLER   *P. sibilatrix*
Regular, though usually rather scarce, on passage

ARCTIC WARBLER   *P. borealis*
Satisfactory notes on 1 near Lluch in July 1967 (RPC)

GOLDCREST   *Regulus regulus*
Irregularly common in winter

FIRECREST   *R. ignicapillus*
Quite common resident

FAN-TAILED WARBLER   *Cisticola juncidis*
Common resident

PIED FLYCATCHER   *Ficedula hypoleuca*
Regular on passage, often quite plentiful

RED-BREASTED FLYCATCHER   *F. parva*
1 at Cabo Formentor, 30/9/1970 (Or)

COLLARED FLYCATCHER   *F. albicollis*
Rare on migration (B)

SPOTTED FLYCATCHER   *Muscicapa striata*
Common summer resident and passage migrant, arriving rather late in spring

WHINCHAT   *Saxicola rubetra*
Fairly common on passage, and occasional summer resident. Breeding suspected (SH et al) and confirmed at Pto Colom, 30/5/1971 (JDP)

STONECHAT   *S. torquata*
Resident, widely distributed in garigue

WHEATEAR   *Oenanthe oenanthe*
Regular on passage in good numbers. The race *O. o. leucorrhoa* moves through in May (DIMW, JDP). *O. o. libanotica* occasionally summers and breeds (B)

BLACK-EARED WHEATEAR   *O. hispanica*
Rather scarce on passage, including both black- and white-throated forms

RUFOUS BUSH CHAT   *Cercotrichas galactotes*
Probably fairly regular on passage, but secretive, and often rather late

ROCK THRUSH *Monticola saxatilis*
Rather irregular on passage, mainly in spring; 3 pairs reported breeding near Soller in 1967 (JGB)

BLUE ROCK THRUSH *M. solitarius*
Resident in fair numbers, mountains and coastal cliffs

BLACK REDSTART *Phoenicurus ochruros*
Common in winter and on passage (early spring)

REDSTART *P. phoenicurus*
Very common on passage

ROBIN *Erithacus rubecula*
Abundant in winter

NIGHTINGALE *Luscinia megarhynchos*
Common summer visitor

BLUETHROAT *Cyanosylvia svecica*
Both the Scandinavian (red-spotted, *C. s. svecica*) and European (white-spotted, *C. s. cyanecula*) races not infrequent on passage in spring, in roughly equal proportions

FIELDFARE *Turdus pilaris*
Irregular in winter: not common

RING OUZEL *T. torquatus*
Occasional in winter, fairly regular on passage. A noticeably pale bird of the race *T. t. alpinus* at Pto Pollensa, 19/3/1967 (JDP)

BLACKBIRD *T. merula*
Widely, but rather thinly, dispersed resident; commoner in winter and on passage

REDWING *T. iliacus*
Quite common, but irregular, in winter

SONG THRUSH *T. philomelas*
Abundant in winter: on passage, often quite late; 1 at Valldemosa, 11/5/1967 (MK, JS)

BEARDED TIT *Panurus biarmicus*
Seen and heard at the Albufera, April 1967 (THE)

MARSH TIT *Parus palustris*
1 near Valldemosa, 9/4/1965 (JDP)

BLUE TIT *P. caeruleus*
Thinly distributed in mountain woods

GREAT TIT *P. major*
Resident in small numbers: may be influxes in winter

PENDULINE TIT *Remiz pendulinus*
1 in reedbed near C'an Pastilla, 18/4/1969
(ARJ)

CORN BUNTING *Emberiza calandra*
Common resident

YELLOWHAMMER *E. citrinella*
Rare visitor (B)

ORTOLAN BUNTING *E. hortulana*
Fairly regular on passage, sometimes in fair numbers

CIRL BUNTING *E. cirlus*
Widespread, rather common resident, and on passage principally in autumn

REED BUNTING *E. schoeniclus*
The race *E. s. witherbyi* is resident in rather small numbers: *E. s. schoeniclus* is
rather more plentiful in winter

CHAFFINCH *Fringilla coelebs*
Widespread resident: also influxes in winter

BRAMBLING *F. montifringilla*
Irregular winter visitor, usually scarce

CITRIL FINCH *Serinus citrinella*
Rare, irruptive. Usually in winter, and has stayed to breed

SERIN *S. serinus*
Very common resident

GREENFINCH *Carduelis chloris*
Common resident

SISKIN *C. spinus*
Irregular winter visitor, and on passage

GOLDFINCH *C. carduelis*
Very common resident

LINNET *Acanthis cannabina*
Common resident

CROSSBILL *Loxia curvirostra balearica*
Endemic race; fairly common resident

HAWFINCH   *Coccothraustes coccothraustes*
Scarce winter visitor (B)

HOUSE SPARROW   *Passer domesticus*
Abundant resident

TREE SPARROW   *P. montanus*
Very occasional on passage, usually spring

ROCK SPARROW   *Petronia petronia*
Resident in small local concentrations

SNOW FINCH   *Montifringilla nivalis*
Recorded in winter by Southern (1955), and possibly 2 more in 1966

STARLING   *Sturnus vulgaris*
Abundant in winter and common on passage: has stayed as late as May

SPOTLESS STARLING   *S. unicolor*
1 in the Albufera, 3/10/1970, and 3 in Bocquer Valley next day (Or). Possibly
overlooked

GOLDEN ORIOLE   *Oriolus oriolus*
Irregular, but not uncommon on passage, mainly in spring

ALPINE CHOUGH   *Pyrrhocorax graculus*
1 in Bocquer Valley, 3/5/1971 (Or)

CHOUGH   *P. pyrrhocorax*
Rare visitor (B). A flock of c 10 small corvids soaring and tumbling near Soller
in April 1965 were chough spp, and others have been suspected

JACKDAW   *Corvus monedula*
2 in Pto Pollensa, 27/9/1971 (Or), would appear to be the first on record

ROOK   *C. frugilegus*
Rare, erratic visitor (B)

RAVEN   *C. corax*
Common in mountains, where it breeds colonially

In addition, the following are now either extinct, rejected, or regarded as open
to doubt:

SLAVONIAN GREBE (*Podiceps auritus*), WHITE-HEADED DUCK (*Oxyura
leucocephala*), WHITE-TAILED EAGLE (*Haliaeutus albicilla*) qv ROCK
PARTRIDGE (*Alectoris graeca*) extinct following introduction in mid-nine-
teenth century, BARBARY PARTRIDGE (*A. barbara*), FRANCOLIN

(*Francolinus francolinus*), DEMOISELLE CRANE (*Anthropoides virgo*), PURPLE GALLINULE (*Porphyrio porphyrio*) extinct, CRESTED COOT (*Fulica cristata*), GREAT SNIPE (*Gallinago media*) probable (M), RED-NECKED PHALA-ROPE (*Phalaropus lobatus*) probable (M), ICELAND GULL (*Larus glaucoides*) probable (M), GUILLEMOT (*Uria aalge*) may be rare offshore, BULLFINCH (*Pyrrhula pyrrhula*) possible escape, CARRION CROW (*Corvus corone*) probable, HOODED CROW (*C. c. cornix*) very probable, but possibility of albinism not excluded

AUTHORITIES

B = Dr F. Bernis. M = Captain P. W. Munn. (See bibliography.)
JSA = Dr J. S. Ash; DGB = D. G. Bell; JGB = J. G. Bellak; BB = B. Brinkhoff; RB = R. Brock; RPC = R. P. Cockbain; CED = C. E. Douglas; RD, PD = Mr and Mrs R. Durman; THE = Mr and Mrs T. H. Ellis; RG = R. Gooding; WG = W. Gubler; SH = S. Holmstadt; ARJ = A. R. Jenkins; MK = M. Kendall; LL = L. Larsen; BL = B. Little; JDM = J. D. Magee; JRM = J. R. Mather; Or = 'Ornitholidays' Ltd; DP = D. Parr; RJP = R. J. Prytherch; JS = J. Sparks; HS = H. Shorrock; HNS = H. N. Southern; DIMW . Mr and Mrs D. I. M. Wallace; WEW = W. E. Waters.

Bibliography

Bernis, F. 'Guion de la Avifauna Balear', *Ardeola*, 4 (1958)

van den Brink, F. H. *A Field Guide to the Mammals of Britain and Europe* (1967)

Colom, G. *El medio y la vida en las Baleares* (Palma de Mallorca, 1964)

Graf, J. *Animal Life in Europe* (1968)

Helmich, W. *Reptiles and Amphibians of Europe* (1962)

Higgins, L. G. and Riley, N. D. *A Field Guide to the Butterflies of Britain and Europe* (1970)

Jeannel, R. *Introduction to Entomology* (1960)

Knoche, H. *Flora Balearica. Etudes phytogéographiques sur les Baléares*, 4 vols (Montpellier, 1923)

Lange, M. and Hora, F. B. *Collins Guide to Mushrooms and Toadstools* (1963)

Munn, P. W. 'The birds of the Balearic Isles', *Novitates Zoologicae*, 37 (1931) and various shorter papers in *Ibis*

Peterson, R. T., Mountfort, G. and Hollom, P. A. D. *A Field Guide to the Birds of Britain and Europe* (1965)

Polunin, O. *Flowers of Europe* (Oxford, 1969)

Polunin, O. and Huxley, A. *Flowers of the Mediterranean* (1967)

Williams, C. B. *Insect Migration* (1958)

Acknowledgements

I HAVE ALREADY made reference to the invaluable help that I have received during the preparation of this work from staff of the BBC Natural History Unit, Bristol—in particular R. Brock, M. Kendall, R. J. Prytherch and J. Sparks. Numerous others who have provided check lists or individual records of birds in particular are named in the Appendix, and to these and the many others who have helped in this way, I extend my most sincere thanks.

In addition, I should like to express my gratitude to the following: the Alpine Garden Society for help with the identification of one or two unfamiliar plants (though the responsibility for all botanical material remains mine alone); Mr T. R. Hedderly, who assisted with my numerous difficulties in translation; and last but by no means least Mrs C. E. Douglas, who spared no pains in tracking down a variety of obscure publications.

Index

In general, English names are given, where possible, in preference to Latin. All plants, butterflies, amphibians, reptiles, mammals and birds (other than the classified entries in the Appendix) are indexed individually, but the less well-known orders of insects, non-flowering plants, etc, are listed collectively.